Shame

JASVINDER SANGHERA

Shame

HODDER &
STOUGHTON

Loughborough College

Copyright © 2007 by Jasvinder Sanghera

First published in Great Britain in 2007 by Hodder & Stoughton
A division of Hodder Headline

A Hodder & Stoughton book

1

A CIP catalogue record for this title is available from the British Library

Hardback ISBN 978 0 340 92460 0
Hardback ISBN 0 340 92460 8

Trade paperback ISBN 978 0 340 92461 7
Trade paperback ISBN 0 340 92461 6

Typeset in Sabon by Hewer Text UK Ltd, Edinburgh
Printed and bound by Clays Ltd, St Ives plc

Hodder Headline's policy is to use papers that are natural, renewable
and recyclable products and made from wood grown in sustainable forests.
The logging and manufacturing processes are expected to conform to
the environmental regulations of the country of origin.

Hodder & Stoughton Ltd
A division of Hodder Headline
338 Euston Road
London NW1 3BH

To Robina, whose life was sadly taken away, and to Mum and Dad, who I now know wanted what they thought to be best for me.

This is my story. However, some of the names and personal information about other people in the book have been changed to protect their identities.

Shame

PROLOGUE

It wasn't too bad in the phone box. It wasn't like the city phone boxes I was used to where you had to hold your breath against the stench of wee and fags. I was glad to be inside it because I'd felt quite conspicuous walking through the village. There were other people wandering about, going up to the pub or buying their tea in the little corner shop, there were kids skidding around on bikes, but there were no other Asian people. Jassey noticed that too, he mentioned it to me. He was leaning up against the wall outside now and I could feel him watching me through the glass. I looked up and smiled at him, pretending I was still fumbling for ten-pence coins in my purse.

I took a deep breath to steady myself. I'd been wanting to make this call for so many weeks now; I'd ached for the sound of familiar voices, for news, for reassurance that all was well. That morning I'd woken up and found the longing was so great I couldn't stand it any longer, I couldn't go another day without speaking to someone from my family. I wanted to talk to my mum, to hear her voice ring with pleasure and relief as she said my name, to know that she and Dad were missing me.

I couldn't admit this to Jassey, but I wanted Mum to tell me to come home. On the drive out from Newcastle I'd had this fantasy that she would say, 'Stay right where you are, *putt*, we're coming to get you.' *Putt* means darling. My dad used to say it to me sometimes. I wished I could hear him say it now. In my imagination I was sitting on the back seat of Dad's old Cortina, Mum looking round to check on me, Dad with his eyes on the road as he drove me safely back to Derby.

I looked at my watch. It was just after seven p.m. I knew Mum would be standing in the kitchen, stirring something on the cooker. I could almost feel the heat and smell the turmeric. Lucy would be in the living-room watching telly. I wondered if the teachers at school had asked her where I was. And Dad would have gone to the foundry. Had he told his friends about me running away? They'd know anyway, of course; in the two months since I'd left home the gossip would have filtered through from our Sikh temple, the *gurdwara*. I hoped I hadn't hurt him too badly. I hoped he missed me as much as I missed him.

Jassey tapped softly on the glass and mouthed 'go on'. I shivered; the evenings were getting cooler and I'd forgotten to bring a jacket. There were goose bumps on my arms and a trickle of cold sweat running down the middle of my back. My heart was beating double time and I could feel the courage draining out of me as I lifted the receiver and fed in the first of my coins.

Mum answered almost immediately. I said, 'Mum, it's me . . .'

She was off straight away, screaming and crying down the phone, and the voice I'd yearned to hear was harsh and shrill. 'What have you done to us? How could you do this? You've shamed us. Why should we suffer this disgrace?'

My dreams of a happy family reunion were instantly shattered. I'd been so stupid. Shame and dishonour were what Mum dreaded more than anything. I should have known she wouldn't forgive me that. But some stubborn part of me was still determined to defend myself. I was crying too by then, but I managed to say, 'Mum, you know why I left.'

But she wouldn't have any of that. The way she saw it I'd defiled the family name by running off with a *chamar*. My mum always told me that *chamars* are the lowest caste, they are the people who pick up dung in the fields; some people call them untouchables. My family are *jats*; back in India *jats* are landowners and no matter that the only land my dad owns in Derby is the patch of grass behind our terraced house, being high caste was a very big thing for us. Through all the shouting and hysterics I couldn't make out if Mum was most cross about my associating with someone of such low birth or the fact that I'd left my intended husband – 'a good match, a *jat*, like us' – in the lurch.

'Thanks to you I can't walk the streets of Derby any more; I can't go to the *gurdwara* because people are talking. People spit at me.' There was a pause; I thought she'd finished but she was just catching her breath. 'You'll get what you deserve for ruining your family. You'll see. In a few months' time you and your *chamar* boyfriend will be rolling round in the gutter which is no more than you deserve. You will amount to nothing, *nothing*, do you hear me? I hope you give birth to a daughter who does to you what you have done to me, then you'll know what it feels like to raise a prostitute.'

I was so shocked by the viciousness of her attack that I was shaking. I couldn't believe it was turning out like this. I wanted her to stop. I wanted more than anything for the conversation to take a better turn, for her to say something – anything – that showed she loved me or even that she cared a little. I wanted her to know that I loved her. My voice was thick with tears.

'I'll come back, Mum. I want to come back. But I won't marry that man. I'm only just sixteen. I want to live my own life. I want to go to college.' I was talking as quickly as I could, trying to get my explanation out, but she started shouting over me and her voice was full of scorn.

'Live your own life then, and good luck to you. In our eyes you're dead!' And with that she slammed the phone down.

My legs seemed to give way beneath me. I was still holding the receiver, staring into it as if I needed visual proof that Mum had cut me off. I slid down the wall and crouched on the floor of the phone box. My chest felt so tight it was as if someone was crushing me. I was literally choking on my sobs. Jassey came in and put his arms around me and tried to comfort me, but for all his kind words and kisses, I had never felt so alone. It was as if someone had taken all my childhood memories and ripped them apart. In the next few days the conversation played over and over in my mind until I thought I would go mad.

'You've shamed us . . .'

'You are dead in our eyes . . .'

'You've shamed us . . .'

'You are dead in our eyes . . .'

Had I really done something so terrible that my parents could disown me? Had they really stopped loving me? Was it such a crime to want my own life?

1

At five-thirty every morning my mum would put her prayers on, full-blast. '*Ik-cum-kar, ik-cum-kar* . . .' The noise went wailing round the house and you couldn't get away from it. You'd put a pillow over your head and think, *stop, p-l-e-a-s-e stop,* but you never blocked it out.

There were four of us in our bed: me, Lucy, Robina and Yasmin, sleeping two at the top and two at the bottom. At bedtime we wriggled and giggled and it was 'you kicked me' and 'move over' and 'that's my space' until we settled down.

There were three other girls in our family. Bachanu, my half-sister, who stayed in India, when Mum came over, Prakash who lived in London, and Ginda, who was about ten years older than me. She slept in the other bed in our room. Ginda was a huge influence in our lives; you could almost say she brought us up. She used to look after us while Mum was at work, and on bath nights she would put us all in the tub together and wash our hair. We all had very long hair, and afterwards she would cover it with jasmine and almond oil which made it greasy and horrible. Your hair would be plastered flat on your head and I hated the feel of that, and the smell. Sometimes, as we got bigger, there wasn't room for all of us in the bath and one person would have to take a bowl of warm water and wash down in the toilet outside. We all dreaded doing that in winter.

Our first house had two bedrooms in it and my brother Balbir slept in the other one. Mum sometimes slept in there too, sometimes downstairs on the sofa. I'd left home before I wondered why there wasn't a bed where she slept with Dad. They must have had a physical relationship: they had seven children together. But there wasn't any sign of it by the time I was old enough to notice; I never saw them kiss one another, not even a peck on the cheek. They didn't seem close; it was just like a practical arrangement. I don't even remember them talking much beyond the questions and answers it takes to get through everyday life.

Balbir was the one who had my mum's attention. He was treated completely differently from us girls. Mum would prepare his food and encourage him to eat it, and she'd wash his clothes, whereas we were expected to wash our own clothes and get our uniforms ready and get our food when we felt like it.

We never all sat down to share a meal. Mum would leave a big pan of curry on the cooker and it was help yourself and take it in front of the TV. We'd sit there cross-legged, balancing our plates on our laps. We had a black and white TV but when we were little we used to spread those transparent Lucozade wrappers across the screen to make it feel like colour.

I was about seven when I started asking why everything was different for Balbir. Why is he allowed out on his own and we're not? Why do I have to learn to cook when he doesn't? Then I started questioning other aspects of our life. If Sikhs think everyone is equal, why do we look down on people of a lower caste?

Just near our house was a *gurdwara*, which was important to my mum because her faith was very strong. Our old house has been knocked down now, but the *gurdwara* is still there, a big red-brick building with silvery domes and tinsel decorations on the front.

Mum left the house at six-thirty every morning and she'd feed the birds on the stretch of grass next to the *gurdwara* and then go in and say her prayers before she went to work. In the evenings she'd go again and she'd bring back holy water and sprinkle it around the house. My sisters and I would be watching *Charlie's Angels* and she'd be sprinkling water all over us and lighting joss sticks and chanting.

The *gurdwara* was – to me still is – the local gossip shop. You see the women standing in huddles with their scarves round their heads.

'Did you know that Zeeta's oldest son has got a wife coming over from the Punjab?'

'Have you heard Hasina's daughter-in-law has had *another* girl? I think Hasina is really regretting that match.'

'What about Zainab Singh? Her mother caught her at the bus stop, talking to a boy. That was three weeks ago and Mira hasn't let her out of the house since. I said to her, "Mira, you have only yourself to blame. Let her mix with white girls and she will pick up white girl ways."'

The worst thing you can say to an Asian girl is that she is behaving like a white person. We weren't allowed to mix with white people because Mum said they didn't have any morals or self-respect. She said whites were dirty people with dirty ways.

That's what all the women I called Aunty thought too, and everyone else in our community. An Asian boy might have a bit of fun with white girls – 'white meat', that's what they'd say – while he was growing up, but when it came to settling down, his family would find him a good Asian bride. If an Asian girl went out with a white boy that was different, that was bad. Her brothers or her uncles would find him and beat him up and then they would beat her too, for bringing shame on the family. Then she would be ruined; no decent Asian man would ever want her. Everyone in the community knew that. I knew it by the time I was eight. No one handed me a book of rules but I knew the particular way in which I was supposed to act, walk, talk, even breathe. I knew that with every bad word said a reputation could die.

We lived in Northumberland Street in Derby. When I was small I used to stand at the top of the street and look down and it seemed so long. All the doors would be open and it was really busy and bustling; people would be wandering from house to house. Now the whole area is Asian, but then it was a very mixed community; there were Asians, Irish and Italian – Pakis, Paddies and Eyeties – all the people that nobody else wanted.

There was a Polish woman we called Mrs Funny and another neighbour we called Mrs Nosey Parker because she was a real curtain-twitcher. We used to play 'Knock out Ginger' on her door. There was an empty house at the top of the street which we told ourselves was haunted; we used to run round it to scare ourselves silly. There were hardly any cars and we played hopscotch and skipping on the pavements and we used to run away from a bad-tempered dog that always seemed to be sitting in the middle of the road. At one o'clock we'd hear the siren from the foundry telling the day shift it was time for their dinner.

My dad worked nights in that foundry. He got his job there on the day I was born, and stayed until he retired. On weekdays I used to make his tea in the morning when he came home; from the age of eight or nine that was my job, and so was sweeping the stairs. We all had jobs, except Balbir of course. In the afternoons when I came home from school I would wake Dad up and pack up his lunch in a steel container like a tower. It had three layers; you'd put different food in each – curry in one, salad in another and chapattis in the third. Mum would make the curries, but I had to do the chapattis.

It used to take me about an hour to make Dad's lunch and his flask of tea. I did it because I loved my dad dearly and doing that for him was a very small thing. I liked sitting with him while he had his tea; sometimes I'd tell him things about my day, but often we just sat, keeping each other company. When it was finished he'd go off to work and I'd stand at the door waiting for him to turn back and wave to me. He always did.

Mum would come in a bit later. She did what work she could get, mostly in textile factories. She always carried a big bag of woven plastic, covered with flowers, and when she came home me and my sisters used to dive for that bag because there was always something nice in it like a sweet or a chocolate. She'd be laughing and saying, 'Let me get in first, let me get my coat off . . .' and we'd all be giggling and grabbing. If I ever got that bag to myself I'd explore it really thoroughly. I didn't want to think I was missing a chocolate. Once I found a tiny little bottle buried right at the bottom and when I took the lid off and smelt it I fell backwards. They were smelling salts and the smell was terrible, it hit the back of your throat and made your eyes water. Mum and my sisters thought that was hilarious.

That bag is the happiest memory I have of childhood with Mum. I don't really remember being close to her. Not in the way my brother was. To me, she was the one that put you in your place and reprimanded you. She didn't like us mucking about or making too much noise and laughing upset her. 'You shouldn't laugh so much, stop that. If you laugh so much you are going to cry.' That's what she used to say.

Of all of us girls I was the tomboy; I loved running in the street and climbing on walls, but if Mum ever saw me she would call me in immediately and I never dared ignore her, I always came straight away. 'Don't you care what people think of you? Are you trying to shame us?' she'd say, holding my shoulders too tightly and peering into my face. 'Seven daughters to bring up . . . that has been my fate. Are you trying to make it harder still? Must you always be different?'

Because I was a breech birth, I was the only one of all Mum's children born in hospital. She spent six days there and she hated it. 'Born with your feet first, pah!' she used to say when she was angry with me. 'You were difficult from the start.'

Her main concern was always that we maintain the family's good name and grow up to be good daughters-in-law who were respectful, subservient and knew how to cook. 'Come here to the stove, stand by me and learn,' she'd say as she got out her cooking pots, and my heart would sink. I remember her recipes now, but those lessons left other, equally vivid memories: my legs aching as I stood beside her, my face hot and flushed by steam, my arm stinging where she slapped me when I let my eyes wander. 'No daughter of mine will go ignorant to her mother-in-law's house.'

Mum was the dominant one in our house. Dad was very quiet and followed what she said. He spent all week working to provide for his family, and then at the weekends he would go to our local pub, the Byron, and get drunk. Sometimes he'd come home happy and sit down in the living-room and ask us to search his hair for nits. We'd all cluster round his chair and he'd sit there telling us jokes and stories as we raked our fingers through his oily black hair, squealing when we caught one and crushed it between our nails. When we were done he'd give us all ten pence pocket money, which doesn't sound like much, but it was a lot for us. Despite the nits, I loved those times because we were all together and even Mum seemed to soften up. She didn't join in but she'd be sat there, watching us all with Dad. It was like our family was the only thing that mattered then, whereas most of the time there would be other people around, aunties and uncles, and Mum would be worrying that we behaved properly in front of them.

Keeping a good face in the community was a very big thing for her. From when we were little she taught us that no matter what was going on in your life you kept your head held high and presented a perfect front. A trouble shared is a trouble talked about by each and every gossip in the *gurdwara*, that's what my mum thought. Better to keep things private and then you can't be judged or shamed.

Sometimes on Saturdays I went with my dad to his allotment. We went up there just the two of us because the others weren't interested. It had huge, rusty iron gates and I would hop out of the car and heave them open so Dad could drive through. He grew potatoes, onions, garlic, marrows, and he showed me how to water them and stake them up. I watched him loosening the soil between his fingers with a faraway look in his eyes and sometimes he started singing softly to himself.

When he was done he sat in his deckchair, smoking a cigarette. Usually he had a can of Tennents lager in the pocket of his coat. That's what made him chatty. I sat beside him on the grass and he told me about his farm in the Punjab and this big shady tree in the middle of his village, Kang Sabhu, where at the end of the day he and the other men used to sit.

'Would I have sat there with you, like I do here?' I said. I knew the answer, we'd had the conversation many times before, but I was relishing the moment, having Dad all to myself. I leant my head against his knees and let his soft, low voice wash over me, filling my mind with exotic images of the life I might have led.

'Goodness me, no. In the daytime, when your chores were done, you might have played under the tree. In fact I remember a rope swing dangling down from one of the branches; as I recall it was Dalbir's son Govind who climbed up to put it there, climbed like a monkey that boy did. You little ones might play there in the day, but in the evening the shade it provided was for the men, it was where we relaxed or, if needs be, discussed the affairs of the village. Your place then was with the women. You would have been minding Lucy, or helping your mother grind the grain. I remember Bachanu when she was only five or six, pulling a wooden stool up to the grain bin which was twice her size and trying to reach down into it with the scoop. She wanted to be like the bigger girls, a helper to her mum.'

'But she couldn't help with the water, could she, Dad.'

'No, *putt*. The pot that your mum took to the well was much too heavy for little girls, it was bronze, you see. If we'd stayed Ginda and Yasmin could do it now, possibly Robina, but you had to be big enough to carry it properly, to lift it up onto your head without spilling any drop.

'Water was precious there. Not like here where you turn on the tap and nobody minds if it runs away useless. Back home we had to carry every drop of water that we used, even the crops weren't irrigated like your uncles' are now. They brought in those irrigation systems two years after I left and I'm telling you it made a difference. I read that productivity has gone sky-high with all that watering.'

His voice was dreamy now and although I could still feel his hand on the back of my head I could tell that in his mind he'd travelled miles away from me. He was back under the big shady tree with his mates.

'You know, I believe that one of your uncles has a tractor now. A mechanical tractor, can you believe that? For us it was ploughs pulled by bullocks. I had some excellent bullocks in my time, but one of them – oh my – that was the most stubborn, obstinate creature ever born and driving him on nearly broke my back.'

'You liked it there, Dad, didn't you. Why didn't you stay?'

This part of the story always made me feel a bit sad. I could picture the great big ship that brought Dad from the Punjab to Liverpool. He and men from other villages round about set off in their crisp cotton shirts and pyjamas, squinting in the bright sunshine as they waved goodbye to their families on the dock. The boat steamed out to sea and by the time India was just a memory lost on the horizon Dad was waking up cold and finding each day was darker than the one before.

He never said this, but I think he found it hard to hold onto his hope as he stood shivering on the deck in the middle of the ocean. He'd told me before that, to cheer themselves up, he and the other men did *bangrha*, a wild traditional dance that was supposed to celebrate the harvest. I couldn't imagine him doing that. In his drab brown clothes he seemed too quiet and serious. I couldn't imagine him wearing earrings either, but he had the holes in his ears.

'Why did you come here, Dad?' I banged the toe of his shoe with the heel of my hand, prompting him to tell the next part of the story.

'It was the 1950s, things were changing, it's always important to keep up to date. I didn't want any son of mine driving a bullock-drawn plough all his life; I dreamt of more for my daughters than the drudgery of carrying water on their heads. Besides the British government was asking us to come, they needed workers, they offered favourable conditions. We were told we would have a wonderful life.'

But what my dad found when he got here wasn't all that wonderful. When he first arrived he shared a house with other Asian men, sometimes as many as twelve crammed into one room. They found it difficult to find places to stay because landlords didn't want to rent to them; there were signs saying NO IRISH, NO BLACKS. They'd come expecting to be welcomed and instead they found hostility. People stopped talking and stared when they went into pubs or shops. Once, my dad was told to get off a bus because he was a Paki. It's not surprising that they stuck together.

Lots of them lived near us in Derby. That's where my mum came to, almost seven years after Dad. She'd married him when she was fifteen; she was told she had to when his first wife, her older sister, died from a snake bite. That was the tradition where they lived. She married her sister's husband and took on Bachanu, her sister's child.

Bachanu was already married by the time Mum came to England, so she stayed behind. What must it have been like for Mum coming all the way to Derby? She never talked about it the way Dad did, but I knew from what he said that before she came to England she'd lived in the same tiny village all her life. She'd never been further than she could walk from that village; she'd never been to town. Before she left the farm my mum had never seen a proper toilet; the only kitchen she had known was in the open air. She never really got the hang of English furniture; when I think of Mum now I think of her sitting cross-legged on the floor, peeling onions.

She must have been lonely when she came here. On the farm she'd have had her in-laws, other women in the house, everybody's kids. When Dad described this household full of people it sounded jolly but I realize now that, more than that, it must have felt safe. Mum would have known her place and her responsibilities; she'd have known where she sat.

I expect she missed that. She didn't know anyone in England. She didn't speak English. She never learnt English, right up until the day she died. Dad learnt enough to get by outside but at home we always spoke Punjabi. We ate Punjabi food, we had Punjabi friends and, although we wore our uniforms to school, we were expected to put on our Indian suits as soon as we came home. It was like you came home and shut the door on Derby and all the white people with their dirty white ways.

Often Dad and I would sit up at the allotment until it was dusk, and as we drove home under the yellow city sky he'd tell me how dark the sky is at night in India and how bright the stars.

Weekends for us were mostly about people coming to our house, or us visiting them. When we went visiting, Ginda used to plait our hair and put ribbons in it and dress us up in really frilly, girly western dresses, like we'd seen the posh kids wear in Asian films. We were so proud of those dresses; mine was green. Once we'd got them on we weren't allowed to go outside or play or do anything except sit still and keep them clean and uncreased so everyone could see how smart we were. The visits were always very formal. The men would be in one room, drinking whisky and smoking, and the women would be in another having the same old conversations.

'Did you see the sari Suki's new daughter-in-law was wearing at the *gurdwara*? So much gold; I hear she is from a rich family. And there she was washing the pots, so she is dutiful too. Suki is very pleased with her.'

'But what of her daughter? Nineteen now and still not married. Why has there been no match?'

'Did you not hear? A match was made, but before the marriage had taken place the groom pulled out because his mother heard that Suki's daughter was dancing with another man at a wedding. Showing herself off. The groom's family wanted nothing more to do with her . . .'

After a while the women would move to the kitchen and continue their gossip while they chopped onions and chillis, ground spices and washed rice. We children were expected to sit quietly or play nicely with whoever was there, but once we were about ten, Mum insisted on us helping to prepare the food because it was a way of showing off what she had taught us, and what good daughters-in-law we were going to make.

2

I came home from my school, St Chad's Infants, one day to find Mum and Ginda in the living-room folding yards of fabric into a big trunk. There were several different pieces in strong, rich colours, some brightly patterned and some covered in embroidery. I'd never seen anything so pretty in our house in my life.

'What's all this for?' I said, reaching out to touch a piece. Mum slapped my hand away. 'It's for Ginda's wedding. She'll be taking it to her new family. It's for her suits.'

'Ginda's getting married? When? Who to?' I looked between the two of them, trying to gauge the mood. Mum looked impassive, you'd think she hadn't heard me. She went on folding fabric, smoothing out the creases until her pile had a perfect surface.

'Who are you marrying, Gin, tell us,' I said.

'His name is Shinda. His picture is on the table over there,' she said, jerking her thumb over her shoulder.

I picked it up. It showed a man a few years older than Ginda, quite good-looking, neatly dressed. 'What's he like?' I said.

'I don't know, I haven't met him, have I, stupid?' she said, and set her mouth firm shut.

That's all the discussion there was. I'd grown up knowing that Ginda would be getting married because it's what all the girls we knew did, but I hadn't expected it to happen so soon. She was only sixteen.

A few weeks later Mum came home from work and said Ginda had gone to India that morning. She didn't say how long she would be gone for and we didn't ask. She was away a month or two and when she came back she was by herself but she was married. That was that. The only word I ever heard about it was one night in our bedroom. The picture I'd first seen of Ginda's husband was lying on our chest of drawers and I picked it up to look at it.

'He doesn't look like that anyway,' she said.

'What do you mean?'

'When I flew out for the wedding he came to meet me at the airport but I didn't recognize him. He doesn't look like that picture at all; I reckon it was doctored.' She rolled over so all I could see was her back and made out she was going to sleep; it was her disappointment and she wasn't going to share it.

Once she was back she went on looking after us like she had before, and she went to work in Reckitt and Coleman's shampoo factory like she had before. Nothing changed for a year or so but then her husband got his papers through and moved to England and she moved out to live with him at his sister's house. That's when I really missed her. All my life she'd looked after me. She could ladle curry out of the saucepan without spilling it, she did our plaits and when Lucy, Robina and I argued, she sorted it out. Sometimes she'd even intervene when Mum was hitting us. That was really brave. She'd reach out and pull me in behind her and in her most soothing, placatory voice she'd say to Mum, 'I think she's learnt her lesson, she'll be a good girl now.' When Ginda left I was eight and I knew I was going to have to fend for myself.

She only went to live ten minutes from us in Depot Street but I didn't see much of her after that except sometimes at weddings. She'd be standing there flanked by her sisters-in-law, all of them queening it in their saris and their jewellery with their eyes darting round like magpies as they checked out all the other women's outfits. She was too engrossed in doing that to talk much to us, but even so I noticed that beneath all her make-up she looked quite down.

Mum and Dad would visit her occasionally on Sundays but it wasn't a regular thing. Ginda was part of her in-laws' family now, that's where her life was and it wouldn't have been right for them to interfere.

It was the same when Yasmin got married. When I was little I thought she might marry the pop man. He used to do deliveries round our street on Sundays and me and Robina thought Yasmin was sweet on him. She'd smooth down her suit and pat her hair when she heard him ring the doorbell and when she answered it she'd lean up against the door frame, all downcast eyes and a coy little smile. But I soon realized that wasn't going to happen. When Yasmin turned sixteen a picture appeared, a trunk got filled, she went away to India for a while then came home married. Her husband was the brother of my eldest sister Prakash's husband and Mum was really pleased about that because it was good to keep things in the family.

Yasmin had the same as Ginda, a ceremony that clinched the deal my parents made so that she could have a proper legal wedding once she'd called her husband over to England. When she came back she still made eyes at the pop man, even though she was supposed to be convincing the immigration officer that she was madly in love with this husband she'd barely met. It took a few months for his papers to come through and then once he'd arrived here she went off to London to stay with Prakash.

By the time I reached my teens I had three sisters married and Robina's husband was already being discussed. If I'd asked Prakash or Ginda or Yasmin if they were happy they would have said yes. That's what was expected of them; if the truth was any different they knew to keep it to themselves. But I didn't like what I saw of their marriages.

You couldn't tell much until the time came when they and their husbands moved into their own houses and, for the first time, they had access to a telephone without all the in-laws listening. They never came round to Dale Road much but they all used to ring. Often, if Lucy, Robina or I answered, whichever one it was would say 'Put Mum on, will you?'

She wouldn't want to chat to us.

'That's what marriage is like . . .'

'Because it's your duty . . .'

'Don't you dare to disgrace us . . .'

'Never mind your father, he would say the same . . .'

That's what the conversation sounded like at our end and when Mum put the phone down she'd be frowning and shaking her head. 'How's Ginda then?' I asked after one of those calls, but Mum just walked past me as if she hadn't heard.

Every few months, Mum would decide it was time to pay a visit and, until we were old enough to be left alone, we had to go with her. Memories of those visits stretch right back into my childhood and none of them are happy memories.

Each one followed the same pattern. Mum chivvied us all into the back of Dad's car. It was his pride and joy, a Ford Cortina. I can still remember how, on hot days, the plastic seating used to stick to my legs. None of us spoke on the drive over and there would be a gathering sense of gloom. The husband would open the front door. He never said anything, just stood back and ushered us all in. My sister – whichever one it was – would be in the living-room, perched on the settee with her baby on her lap. The husband and Dad disappeared into the other room and Mum sat down opposite my sister while the rest of us sat cross-legged by the wall. I knew what was coming and I didn't want to hear it. I wished we could go and play in another room but I was afraid to ask; I knew better than to draw attention to myself at a time like this.

'What's all this about then?' Mum said, sounding stern rather than sympathetic.

My sisters never needed encouragement. 'I can't stand it any longer. He is a difficult man.' The complaints would come, of various incidents and conflicts. 'Baby was crying while we were eating, I wanted to go to him, but he wouldn't let me. Yesterday he shouted at me because he said his dinner wasn't hot. What can I do? Every day there's something. Why should I put up with it?'

'Because you are his wife,' said Mum, and by now there would be a sharp, don't-mess-with-me edge to her voice. She never shouted on these occasions but when she brought out that tone we knew exactly who was boss. 'It is your duty to look after your husband and to please him.'

'But he gets so angry.'

'This is his house, he can behave as he wishes. Stop that crying, crying does no good. You must learn how to calm him.'

'But I don't see why . . .'

'It is not your duty to see. It is your duty to have a respectable marriage and to uphold the good name of your family. That is the very least that your father and I expect. Do you understand that?'

It was always hot and stuffy in those rooms, the babies were heavy and my legs would ache from sitting cross-legged but I never dared fidget. I jiggled the babies if they got fractious. Lucy pulled faces at them trying to make them smile.

Mum was more than a match for her daughters. They soon stopped trying to make themselves heard and sank back into the corner of the settee, twisting their handkerchiefs in their laps as tears rolled down their cheeks.

Then Mum called the men in. She pushed the son-in-law over to sit by his wife, and told Dad to sit down next to her. Dad never said anything on these occasions, only sometimes he nodded his head as if in agreement. Perhaps he was wishing he could escape to the Byron. A couple of times he would get out his cigarette pack and make as if to light one, but then he would look at Mum and put it back again. She didn't let him smoke indoors.

When Mum turned her attention to the husband, her tone was gentler and more wheedling. 'You can see she is trying, but it is hard for her away from her family. Perhaps you could try to be more patient with her. She has given you a lovely boy and if you are blessed perhaps there will soon be another. You must think of your family now. No good will come to your son if his mother is always crying.'

The sons-in-law never looked at her while she was speaking; they kept their heads bowed down so they missed her obsequious smiles. It wasn't until Mum had finished talking that any of them ever met her gaze and then even I could tell their eyes were insolent. You could see the corners of their mouths twitching as they said, 'Yes, *Bibi-ji.*' *Bibi* means mother and *ji* is something you add to the name of anyone above you. It's a mark of respect, but my brothers-in-law didn't sound respectful. They weren't afraid of Mum. She'd said what she'd come to say and they knew she'd never take it any further for fear of creating a wrinkle in our family's reputation.

We were all quiet on the way home. The only sound in the car was Dad muttering to himself. If you were sitting behind him you could see his head moving about as though he was having a conversation with himself, going through everything that had happened. I don't think he was happy with those meetings, but he'd never interfere with what Mum said.

She'd always sit still in the car looking straight ahead of her. It wasn't until we were turning into our road that she used to twist round in her seat so she was facing us. 'There's no need to talk of this with anybody. Not even your aunties. It is a private matter for our family. Do you understand that? I won't have people talking about us, I won't have you giving people reason to gossip in the *gurdwara.*'

3

The year that Ginda got married we moved house. Dale Road was just round the corner from Northumberland Street, but it was a step up. The new house had three bedrooms, a proper bathroom and an inside toilet. It was luxury for us. It was so close to our old house that we carried most of our stuff round by hand. Some of Dad's friends from the factory helped with the furniture and I remember Mum walking down the street with a big case balanced on her head and me, Lucy, Robina and Yasmin all trailing along behind her carrying bits and pieces. Lots of our neighbours came out of doors to watch and it felt a bit like a procession.

We four girls were still sharing a room but Balbir had his own room again in Dale Road. He was doing an apprenticeship in engineering by then but that didn't stop him going out at nights. He used to come home late and put his music on really loud. Bob Marley was what he liked: 'No Woman No Cry', 'I Shot the Sheriff', 'Satisfy My Soul', 'Get Up, Stand Up' . . . Night after night those songs blasted round the house waking us up.

'Shut up, Balbir. Turn it down. We're trying to sleep,' we shouted from the bedroom but he couldn't hear us above the racket. It was Mum who heard us and she came into our room with a face like thunder as though we were the noisy ones.

'Stop shouting!' she'd say. 'Be quiet and go to sleep.'

'But Mum. It's impossible to sleep with Balbir's music. It's him, tell him to stop.'

'You leave your brother out of this. I'm telling you, shut up and go to sleep.'

One night I got so cross I decided to sort him out myself. I kicked back the blanket and stamped down the passage. There he was, bedroom door wide open, playing air guitar and caterwauling along with the lyrics. He looked so ridiculous I almost laughed.

'Can't you think of other people for a change, we've got school in the morning,' I shouted above his screeching. He didn't even stop twanging his pretend guitar, just aimed a kick in my direction. It wasn't hard, but dodging to avoid it I fell back through the door and landed practically on top of Mum, who was coming up the stairs. She steadied me and then gave me a shove back towards our bedroom.

'Get back to bed, young lady. You've no business here,' she said.

Next morning when we were getting ready I thought Robina was taking too long in the bathroom. I was rattling the door handle and calling through to her to hurry up when Mum appeared behind me, making shushing noises.

'Keep your voice down, your brother is sleeping. Have a bit of consideration, he's a working man now, bringing home money. He needs his sleep.'

*   *   *

When I was ten or eleven Balbir started going out with Dawn, who lived just round the corner from us on Darby Street. Dawn's dad was Asian but her mum was a white woman and our mum didn't like that; she called Dawn a half-caste. She was always going round to Dawn's house and hammering on the door, demanding to know if Balbir was in there. Sometimes she'd take me with her so I could shout the words in English. Once she made me say that something terrible would happen if Dawn didn't stop seeing Balbir but she didn't take a blind bit of notice. Nor did Balbir. He knew Mum would never really go against him.

After one of those trips I asked her why she didn't *make* Balbir stop seeing Dawn and stay at home. 'You wouldn't let my sisters do what he does, why is he different?' I didn't mean to be cheeky, I wanted an answer, but that's not how she saw it.

'Insolent child.' She stooped to take off her shoe and, grabbing my tunic so I couldn't slip away from her, started beating me with it. She didn't mind where the blows landed – legs, back, head – I'm not sure she even noticed, she was so worked up with her shouting. 'Don't question me, of all my daughters you alone are difficult, always thinking you know best . . .'

One new thing Dad had in Dale Road was a shed. It was part of the house really, a sort of add-on to the kitchen, but we always called it Dad's shed because it was where he kept his gardening tools and where he stored the onions and potatoes that he'd grown. We used to climb on top of the shed when we were playing *Charlie's Angels*, and sometimes I'd sit up on the roof by myself and pretend I was guarding Dad's stuff. I was always looking for ways to make myself special to Dad. Out of all of us Balbir was the important one because he was the only boy and that's how it goes in Asian families; I knew that but I still liked to think the bond between me and Dad was different. We had a secret anyway.

It happened one night when I woke up so thirsty that I went downstairs to get a drink of water. I was treading carefully on the stairs so I didn't make them creak when I heard the sound of voices, men's voices whispering and laughing softly. It was coming from the shed. Usually it smelt dusty and dry but that night as I stepped into the kitchen I could smell something different, something sickly sweet and horrible. It was a smell I thought I recognized.

Suddenly the shed door opened and Dad came into the kitchen. He was carrying a couple of empty milk bottles and talking over his shoulder to his friends as he headed for the sink to fill them from the tap. When he caught sight of me he whipped round, quick as a flash. He had a really guilty expression on his face and he leant over to push the shed door shut before saying gently, 'Go back to bed, *putt*, it's late, you need to sleep.'

'What are you doing, Dad? What's that smell? Who's in the shed?'

'It's nothing for you. Don't worry about it, go back to bed.' He was trying to block my path with his body, but I was peering round him. The shed door had swung open and I could see two of Dad's friends, men I referred to as 'uncle', standing in the dim light.

'What are you doing, Dad? What are my uncles doing here?'

He sighed, then smiled. 'Okay, come and see. We are making Desi.'

The concrete floor of the shed was cold beneath my bare feet; I shivered. The tiny space was filled with acrid steam which made my eyes smart. I pinched my nose to block the smell. One of Mum's big saucepans was balanced on a gas canister and the liquid inside it was bubbling like anything. There were packets and bags and spoons on the floor beside it and, lined up against the wall, a row of empty bottles. Suddenly I realised what the smell was: aniseed. A couple of years back, attracted by the colour, I'd bought little red balls of it from the sweet shop. They were revolting.

'This is Asian alcohol, good strong stuff,' Dad said, and he and the other men laughed. He dipped a ladle into the saucepan and filled a small glass with the clear liquid. 'Watch this,' he said, striking a match and wafting it across the top of the glass. To my amazement it caught light. The greeny-blue flame rose and danced, casting flickering shadows on our faces. Then it sputtered and died. Once it was out Dad and my uncles passed the glass round and they all had a taste.

'Can I try it, Dad?' I said, and the men laughed again.

'No, child, Desi is not for little girls. Now you've seen it, Jasvinder, go back to bed!'

When the time came to leave Dale Primary I went to join Robina and Yasmin at Littleover School. It was too far to walk there so when Dad came back from the night shift he used to stay up, drinking tea and reading his paper, until it was time to give us all a lift. I can remember him standing at the bottom of the stairs and shouting up to us: 'Lucy! Jasvinder! Neddy!' – that's what we called Robina when she was young. 'Come on, it's time to get up. Wash your face, brush your teeth and come. Quick!'

He'd stand there, shouting for us until we came down like a swarm of bees, grabbing a couple of biscuits for our breakfast, looking for our school books, fighting about whose turn it was in the front of the car.

It was about two miles from our house to Littleover and Dad always took the same route. He went along Dale Road, then Cavendish and after the roundabout at the end, he turned into a great long road called Warwick Avenue. We were still in the Asian area, but this was the smart bit.

Warwick Avenue is wide, it has trees planted on both sides and it is lined with huge old Victorian houses, beautiful houses with front gardens and off-street parking. I used to crane out of the window and imagine myself living there. I'd see myself getting out of bed – my own bed – onto a thick pile carpet, or watching the telly sitting on a big soft sofa, or opening the front door and stepping out onto my own green lawn.

'One day I'm going to buy a house on this road, you know, Dad,' I said.

I was sitting next to him in the front and he turned to me and smiled indulgently. 'Course you are, *putt*, one day.'

'I am, Dad. Believe me, I will one day.'

'Oh yeah.' 'Very likely.' 'Buy two, why don't you?' said my sisters in a sarcastic chorus from the back.

4

When I was thirteen I got my first job with the newsagent at the bottom of Northumberland Street. I was paid £5.25 a week for delivering the papers to about eight streets round us. The bag was heavy and my shoulder used to ache but I loved doing it. It wasn't for the money. I used to give that to Mum. She never said I had to, but I knew that was what she expected: I'd seen my sisters saving money to bring their husbands over. I'd say, 'Here you are, Mum,' and she would count it carefully and sometimes she'd pat me on the head before putting the coins in the jar behind the cooker.

I loved the freedom. The paper round was the only time I was allowed out on my own. If you were sent to the corner shop to buy something you had to get there and back within ten minutes. After school we had to come straight home. Mum never came to school – she never went to parents' evenings or talked to teachers – but she knew exactly how far away it was and if I walked through the door fifteen minutes later than I should have done I was for it. If she wasn't there to see for herself my sisters always told her. It was the same for all of us. If an aunty saw you dawdling in the street or talking to a friend she'd tell Mum. The paper round was like a liberation. In the winter I had to hurry to keep warm but on sunny summer Saturdays I'd saunter up and down those streets taking the longest route I could. I looked at the white girls hanging around in little groups, leaning up against the lampposts, showing off their tight jeans. I longed to have a pair.

'What are you thinking of? Why would you want to go round showing off your bum? Have you no shame, girl?' Mum said when I asked her.

Working was part of our lives once we reached adolescence. One summer holidays Mum got me a job in a pickling factory. She said not to say how old I was but the supervisor was a friend of hers and I don't think he minded me being under age. It was only for a couple of weeks anyway. I can't remember much about it except the mind-numbing boredom of the work and the way the smell of pickles clung to your clothes and your hair. I tried to train myself to breathe through my mouth until I could get home and wash myself.

The only good thing about that job was Avtar; she was the girl next to me on the line and once I'd got my part of the production process off pat we could talk while we worked. Avtar was a free spirit and she made me laugh. She stayed at the factory after I left but we kept in touch and, as it turned out, knowing her would later change my life.

In the meantime I got another job, in Presto, which was about ten minutes' walk from our house. I did two evenings a week, sitting on the checkout or filling the shelves. Over my clothes I had to wear a pale blue nylon pinafore with Presto embroidered on it and I got paid £12.50 a week but I told Mum it was £11.50 and kept the extra £1 a week for myself. I had to unseal my wage packet to get the money out and at first my hands used to shake, I was so scared of tearing it, but I soon became quite clever at it and Mum never guessed. I wanted the money to pay to have my hair cut; it took me almost three months to save up enough.

I was fourteen and a half but I'd never had my hair cut. Ever. Mum or Ginda occasionally trimmed the split ends but that was all and by the time I was fourteen my hair hung down below my bottom which was just how Mum wanted it. Short hair was for white girls with their fast western ways. Good Punjabi girls wore their hair in plaits.

That spring the fashion was for wild curls. In the dinner break at school my white friend Caroline and I used to sit with our backs against the fence and study the pictures in her copies of *Jackie* and *Just Seventeen*. Caroline had straight hair like me but she said her mum was going to let her have a perm. I knew Mum would never let me; I wouldn't even dare to mention it.

There was a hairdresser called Rafferty's just near Presto and its window was full of pictures of all the different hairstyles you could have. I used to stop on the way to and from work and gaze at the picture of the girl with curled hair. It was cut just above her shoulders, tumbling this way and that, and I thought she looked fabulous. I'd stare in at the window and dream of looking just like she did. One afternoon I set off for work ten minutes early and, having checked that no one Mum knew was passing, I plucked up the courage to go in.

The woman at the desk was talking on the phone and she didn't look up. I stood there waiting, glancing out the window every few seconds to check no one had seen me come inside. Eventually she finished her call and said, 'Yes?'

'How much would it cost to have my hair done like this?' I asked, moving over to the window and pointing at 'my' picture.

She came out from behind the desk, went over to the window, and stuck her head round so she could see which one it was. Then she consulted a list of prices on the desk. It felt like she took ten minutes but it can't have been long.

'Cut and perm costs nine pounds fifty. Do you want an appointment?'

'Can I come next Saturday?'

'Morning or afternoon?'

'Either. After ten o'clock.'

'Twelve-thirty, then. Name?' she said, and when I'd spelt it out for her she closed her book. I ran all the way to Presto and my heart was pumping fast.

Saturday morning came and I was up early, anxious to check that Mum and Dad were going out. They were supposed to be visiting Aunty Rajni in Stoke, but I was fretting that they'd change their minds. It seemed to take Mum ages to get ready, fussing about the pot of dhal she was taking, losing her glasses in her big flowery bag. Dad stood in the doorway smoking a cigarette and reading the paper. When they finally climbed into the old Ford Cortina and drove away I was so relieved I felt light-headed.

A couple of hours later I ran down the stairs. Robina had gone out to her Saturday job. She'd already been to India for her marriage and now, while she finished school, she was saving hard to bring her husband over. It was just Lucy in the living-room; she'd been in there since *Tiswas* came on the telly.

'I'm going out,' I called, without slowing my pace, and the door slammed shut behind me before she could ask where.

Everything in Rafferty's was new to me. The beige nylon gown they put you in. The adjustable chair. The enormous mirror right in front of you. Rod Stewart's 'Do Ya Think I'm Sexy' was blaring out and everyone seemed to be chatting; I began to relax and enjoy myself. I'd shaken my plait out just before I left Dale Road and now one of the hairdressers was pulling her comb through my hair, running it right through from top to bottom.

'Gorgeous thick hair you've got, love. Just a trim, is it?' she asked.

'No. I want it like that picture in the window. The one in the middle.'

She dropped my hair and, just as the receptionist had, walked over to the window and peered at the picture. Watching her as she headed back towards me, I could see she looked surprised.

'You want it permed?'

I nodded.

'Not many . . .' she faltered before closing her mouth on the word Pakis, and after a second went on, 'girls like you do that. Seems a shame when you've got this lovely long hair.'

'It's what I want,' I said firmly.

'Here we go then,' she said. 'First we've got to lose at least half of it.'

I watched, fascinated, as she pinned up hanks of hair and then got her scissors out. Within seconds lengths of hair lay coiled round my chair like fat black cobras. I didn't feel a second's regret. I was revelling in how cool and light my head felt. Abba's 'Mamma Mia' was playing now and it was all I could do to stop dancing in my seat.

My hairdresser was talking all the time, not to me, but to another woman working next to her. They were discussing a nightclub they were both going to that night. But it didn't seem to slow her down. Her scissors moved through my hair like quicksilver, snipping this way and that. Once the length was right she drenched my hair in a solution which smelt foul and caught the back of my throat; then she went to work with her rollers. When she was done it looked like I had pink hedgehogs all over my head. That was the only time I wondered what I'd let myself in for.

But I needn't have worried. When the hairdresser finally put her brush down and stood back to admire her handiwork I couldn't stop myself; I grinned at my reflection with delight. My hair stopped just above my shoulders; she must have cut off eighteen inches, and it was soft curls everywhere. I loved it.

I tried to sneak back into Dale Road but Lucy saw me. She stopped dead in her tracks and her mouth dropped open.

'You're gonna get it when Mum sees you,' she said, her eyes round as gobstoppers. 'Robina, come and look, Jas has cut her hair off and it's gone all curly.'

I enjoyed the reaction but I knew she was right. Mum would be furious. The thought of her rage almost took the pleasure out of looking at my new reflection in the mirror. I decided I had to keep it from her. When she and Dad came home from Aunty Rajni's I had my head wrapped up in a towel, as if I'd just had a bath and washed my hair.

'Night, Mum,' I called, all innocent as I went up early to bed.

For the next three days I kept out of her way and made sure that, whenever I was in the house, I had a towel on my head. My heart used to beat that bit faster when I heard Mum's footsteps approaching, and I could feel the tension growing in Lucy and Robina as they waited for the blow-up. It came on day four. I went into the kitchen to fetch myself a drink and I could tell from the way Mum looked at me that she was suspicious. As I walked past her to the sink she turned from the cooker and twitched the towel off my head.

For a second we stood staring at each other. It was as if Mum was frozen; her face was like a mask of horror. Then she snapped out of it, grabbed my arm and launched herself at me like a crazy person. Her first blow hit me on the head; I lurched backwards and hit the counter, knocking a saucepan that was waiting to be washed. It fell to the floor with a clatter and its lid spun off and rolled round the kitchen floor with a clanging that resounded with the ringing in my head. Mum was raining blows down on me and shouting, 'What have you done, girl? Again you have shamed us. What were you thinking of? You think you are clever with your western ways but no decent man will want you now. Will you not be happy until you have dragged us all down into the gutter.' I was shielding my face with the arm she wasn't holding and trying to twist away from her, but with each question she landed a wallop, harder and harder as she worked herself up.

I tried to interrupt, to reason with her. 'Mum, it's only a haircut. It'll grow out again. Why does it matter?'

But I could hardly make myself heard above her shouting, incoherent now her voice was broken with accusatory sobs. 'Do you want to make yourself look cheap like the white girls? Do you want them talking about you in the *gurdwara*? Was it your plan to bring shame on your family?'

She was breathing heavily, a big woman tired by her exertions. Unconsciously, she let go of my arm to sweep her hair back off her face; I heard the deep intake of breath as she prepared to resume her tirade but I didn't stay to hear the rest. Seizing my opportunity, I darted beneath her raised arm and fled the kitchen, squeezing past Robina and Lucy, who were standing wide-eyed in the doorway. As I ran upstairs I could hear Mum wailing still. 'I am burdened with seven daughters, why must this one bring nothing but trouble? Why must I suffer this? What can I do with this girl?'

Two days later I was doing my shift in Presto, re-stocking the shelves with beans, when a figure suddenly strode down the aisle, grabbed the back of my hair and started shouting at me.

'What is this, you foolish girl? What have you done? Are you trying to disgrace us all?'

It was my sister Prakash, come all the way from London to inspect my haircut. I couldn't believe it. I was mortified but I was also scared. We were all scared of Prakash.

'Get off me,' I hissed, glancing round to see if anyone was watching us. 'Be quiet. Please. You can't shout at me in here.'

'I can teach you to have some respect. You'll see, young lady,' she said and, to my relief, she turned on her heel and stalked out.

She was there at Dale Road when I got back. Mum called out immediately.

'Come in here, Jasvinder. I want to tell you something.'

I stood in the doorway, hesitant. She and Prakash were looking very stern. 'When your sister goes back to London tomorrow morning you will go with her,' Mum said. 'Here you are dishonouring your family, picking up western ways. I can't control you and Prakash needs some help in the house. You can go and learn what it is to be a dutiful daughter.'

Prakash, sitting beside her, nodded her head and looked smug. The prospect of living with her – and worse still her drunken husband – was terrible.

'How long will I go for, Mum?'

'We'll see.'

'But I'll be back in time for school, yeah?'

She didn't answer. I felt my chest tighten with a mixture of panic and anger. School was my link with the wider world, my escape.

'You'll be in trouble if you keep me off school. You're not allowed to, that's the law in England. Remember what the truant officer said last time you did.'

But she and Prakash had turned away. The punishment meted out, they had turned their attention to something else.

It must have been about three months I stayed with Prakash, long enough for my perm to fall out and my hair to grow back long enough to plait. Mum wanted me decent before I could be seen again in Derby. It was an awful time. The days were monotonous and each one felt endless. My big sister seemed to enjoy the task of teaching me respect. As soon as I got there she took away my one western skirt – it was well below the knee – and blouse and made me always wear Indian suits, dreadful things she'd made herself. But it didn't matter what I wore because I wasn't allowed to go anywhere except a tiny little park near the house where I sometimes took the children. They were my salvation. Her three boys Ranjit, Manjit and Baljit were all under twelve then and I enjoyed playing with them, when I was allowed to do so.

Most of my time was spent helping Prakash with her job, which was sewing ties. When I think of Prakash I think of her sitting at her sewing machine, day and night. She sewed the ties inside out and my job was to turn them right way round again, using a long stick. Then I had to iron them. The children had to help with the turning too when they came home from school, and if they didn't work fast enough Prakash would get angry.

As well as helping with the ties I had to do household chores, cooking and cleaning, cleaning and cooking. Prakash never seemed to run out of jobs for me. The evenings and the weekends were the worst because then her husband, Bila, was there, throwing his weight about, stinking of whisky. His eyes were yellow, which I used to tell myself meant he was a devil. I later learnt it was a symptom of the liver poisoning that finally killed him. He shouted at Prakash and shoved or slapped her if she didn't anticipate his every need. He was a bully and I hated him.

It was October and half the school term had gone by before Mum and Dad appeared at the house. I was so pleased to see Dad that I rushed across the room to hug him. He didn't know what to do. He stood there with his arms dangling by his sides, but he was laughing as he said very gently, 'All right, *putt*, all right.' Mum was strict as ever. At first I didn't know if she was going to let me come home but after she'd been there a bit she said, 'Have you learnt your lesson? Are you going to behave if we take you back to Derby? If you don't you'll be coming straight back.' That's when I knew my punishment was over.

5

A few months after Mum brought me home from Prakash's house the subject of my marriage came up. I was in the living-room doing my homework when she showed me a picture, ever so casually. 'What do you think of him?' she said. 'Do you think he's nice? He's the man you're going to marry.' I must have known this moment would come but I still felt as if I had been slapped. I didn't want to look at the picture, in my head I didn't want to go there, but I couldn't stop myself taking a quick glance. She was pointing out a man standing in a group and my first thought was, no way am I marrying him, *he's shorter than me*. I just looked at Mum. Then she started laughing and put the picture away so I thought perhaps she was joking and I needn't take it seriously.

I tried to put it to the back of my mind and get on with my life, but every so often Mum would mention it. At first she was always light-hearted and jokey, but over the weeks she became more insistent. She kept saying I should be happy that she had found me such a good husband and that it was my duty to marry him. As the weeks went by I got more and more frightened. I kept thinking of my sisters and the bruises I'd seen on them; I remembered them sobbing as they told my parents how their husbands abused them; I remembered Mum saying, 'This is how men are, it is your duty to look after him.' I used to lie awake and dread the thought of my husband beating me, and Mum and Dad refusing to help. I felt as if my life were sliding out of my control. When I said, 'Mum, I want to finish school and go to university,' she just laughed.

At break times at school I'd watch the white girls. It was a style thing then for them to hitch their uniforms up so they were really short. I used to watch them, standing in groups with the boys, chatting and laughing, sometimes mock wrestling; occasionally a cheeky couple would even kiss. For them it was totally normal, but my mum would have killed me if she saw me doing that.

My white friends had started talking about going to college or university. When they said, 'Is it true you have to get married when you're really young?' I'd just say no. I used to wonder if other Asian girls in my class were going through the same thing as me, but I never dared ask them because I'd been so indoctrinated not to talk outside the family. Sometimes I used to fantasize about telling a teacher and asking them to help, but it would have flown in the face of everything Mum ever taught me. My fear of being judged was quite deeply ingrained by then.

Even if I had been brave enough to tell a teacher, I didn't think they'd understand. Robina stayed in India six months when she went to have her marriage and when she came back the teachers never even asked her where she'd been or why, they just put her down a year because she'd missed so much school work. Anyway I was ashamed to tell anyone that my mum was arranging my marriage while I was still at school. And I was afraid of what my family would do to me, and what the rest of the community would say about them if I did.

No matter that I was so reluctant, the arrangements for my wedding were soon well under way. The photograph of the man I was supposed to marry was on the mantelpiece, leering down at me when I came home from school. I'd studied it more closely by then: he was ugly as well as short, he looked much older than me and he had a stupid haircut. I still didn't know his name, no one ever bothered to tell me that. More and more often, I'd come back and find that Mum had been out shopping. Gradually the chest that would go with me to my husband's family was being filled up. Mum even bought my wedding dress without me, a red glittery thing that I refused to look at. She couldn't care less that I didn't want to get married; she had already married five daughters and she didn't see why I should be any different. Ginda and Yasmin backed her up; they used to say, '*Teri fol laga ya*,' which means, 'Why are you any different, have you got flowers attached to you?'

Even Robina was on their side. 'Just do it. It's what we've all done,' she said. She was keen on the match because her husband, Navtej Sanghera, was friends with the man I was supposed to marry and came from the same part of India. Since her application for Navtej to come to England had been rejected, he'd moved to Germany and she was joining him in Frankfurt as soon as she had saved some money to take with her. 'Your husband is going to Frankfurt too, Navtej told me. If you get married there we will be together,' she said.

She sounded light-hearted but my mind flashed back to a night not long before she left to meet her husband. She'd gone missing. At first Mum thought she'd slipped out to meet a friend and she was angry. But about ten o'clock Dad went out into the garden for a cigarette and he found Robina there, hiding behind the shed. He called Mum out and the three of them stood in a huddle. I could hear Robina sobbing and a couple of times she cried out 'Please'. Eventually they all came in looking grim and later on, when we were in bed, Robina whispered that she'd been hiding because she was scared of getting married.

Dad didn't say much about my marriage. He was the only one who might have persuaded me to go through with it because I loved him and I believed he loved me. But he left it up to Mum. Sometimes when he'd had a drink – he was always more talkative when he came back from the Byron – he'd stroke my cheek and say, 'Come on, *putt*. Don't try to fight this, it's what we all do.' But it wasn't enough. He didn't try hard enough.

Mum more than made up for it. She was always one for superstitions, things like if you sneeze before leaving the house you have to go back in and eat something sweet. Now she got it into her head that someone had put a spell on me.

'I'm telling you, Chanan, the child is possessed. Someone has cursed her and my suspicion falls on that old man who sits on the corner by the *gurdwara*. You've seen him? Straggling beard and unwashed clothes. Well, what is he doing there if not causing trouble?'

I was doing my homework – it was maths and we were working on Venn diagrams, I can remember that because I liked the clear simplicity of them. I got up from the table and went to the kitchen door to listen. I peeped round in time to see Dad's head start its little nodding dance. He wanted to show Mum that he was listening, weighing up the situation. She had her back to me, stood there in front of him, hands on her hips as she continued.

'Her behaviour is not normal. Why would she be so difficult if she were not possessed? She needs ridding of those demons and I think I've found someone to do it.' Suddenly she dropped her voice and bent forward to whisper conspiratorially. I strained to hear but I could only catch the odd word, 'Hindu', 'demons', 'Thursday'. I was craning forward at the door but I jumped back as she straightened up and said in her normal voice, 'This is between the two of us, Chanan, I'm not going to tell the other girls.'

She didn't mention anything to me, but the following Thursday when I got home from school she was ready waiting by the door, with a headscarf that I'd never seen before wrapped close around her head. I'd barely had time to put my bag down when she handed me a scarf, helped me draw it round my face and hustled me back out.

'Where are we going, Mum?' I said as she linked her arm through mine and hurried me down the pavement. Her eyes were glued to the ground and she didn't lift them or turn towards me as she said, 'You'll know soon enough. Quick now, and don't look about.' We stopped at a Hindu temple about twenty minutes' walk from our house. Mum wouldn't have risked being seen in our area.

The Hindu priest who was supposedly going to cast out my demons was really old and he had this great long beard; he was wearing a skirt thing and a baggy top. He asked Mum my date and time of birth and all my likes and dislikes and then he started wringing his hands and saying, 'We must calm this troubled spirit.'

I just sat there dumbly as he ranted on, spouting off at me in

Punjabi. 'This is your fate and if you ignore it your family will suffer and you will meet with terrible misfortune. Ignore your duty at your peril.' Mum had obviously filled him in on the whole situation beforehand.

Before we left, he gave me this dark green bottle of what he called medicine and said I had to drink some twice a day. It was supposed to bring me to my senses. Any fool could tell it was only sugared water, but it made Mum happy if I drank it so I did.

She went about her preparations with new enthusiasm. I'd come home from school and find her refolding my fabrics, checking that each crease was perfect. She started making a new suit for herself so I guessed that she'd be coming with me. Watching her felt so strange, like looking at my life through the wrong end of a telescope. She was planning my wedding but the plans were moving independently of me. I tried to ignore them, to blank them out. I had to control myself or the fear trembling in my belly would rise up and block my throat.

One night it all got too much. I came into the living-room and Mum was there with Ginda and one of my aunties and they were all standing over the chest, admiring the wedding fabrics. Suddenly it seemed so real and close that I knew I had to do something. I said, 'Mum, I'm not getting married. I'm going to finish school and go to college.'

Mum was so angry that I could speak to her like that in front of an outsider – disrespectful and blabbing about the troubles in our family – that she picked up her heavy sewing scissors and whacked me really hard on the arm. She was screaming and crying and saying to my auntie, 'Look what I have to put up with; I have to carry the burden of seven daughters and this one has no shame,' and my auntie was crying as well and saying, 'You must be a good girl and do this for your family, look how you are upsetting your mother,' and I started crying and I stormed out, slamming the door.

The next night I was stopping at Ginda's. Mum used to send me there occasionally: 'Go and stay with your sister, and while you are there see if you can find some sense!' When I was younger I used to like going. I'd always enjoyed having Gin all to myself, but nowadays there were awkward silences between us. She wouldn't talk about my marriage. What was the point? As far as Gin was concerned it was inevitable and there was nothing to discuss.

I felt she had abandoned me. Gin virtually brought me up. She used to bath me when I was little. She reassured me when I got my first period and sorted me out; Mum had never mentioned it. She'd told me what little I knew about the facts of life. Now, it seemed, she was too caught up in her duty and the community and the family's reputation to care about me. I went upstairs that night feeling really upset and angry. I felt I was screaming my lungs out trapped in a soundproofed box.

In Ginda's bathroom there was a shelf above the bath where she kept her shampoo and face cream, stuff like that. There was a bottle of paracetamol on it and that night, on impulse, I picked it up and unscrewed the lid. A second or two passed and then I shook a couple of tablets into my hand, and a couple more, and a couple more after that. How many were there in the end. Eight? Ten? I don't know. I looked down into my palm and instead of little white pills what I saw was an image of Mum, crying and beating her breast. I shoved the pills into my mouth and then stuck my head under the tap and took a great draught of water; and another. Then I left the bathroom and went and got into bed.

I lay there for a while monitoring myself for any little symptom. After about ten minutes I started feeling sick and frightened. I got out of bed and crept downstairs to the living-room where Gin was watching telly.

'Gin?' I whispered.

She cocked her head towards me without taking her eyes off the screen.

'Gin, I think I've taken too many paracetamol. I don't feel good.'

She whipped round. 'What do you mean, stupid girl. How many have you taken? Is the bottle empty?' She leapt up, grabbed me by the shoulders and peered into my face as if the appearance of my eyes and skin might give her the answer. 'You *stupid* girl, I must go for help,' she said and, letting go of me, she hurried from the room.

I could hear her hammering on her neighbour's door then a murmured conversation and, minutes later, she reappeared with a woman called Eileen. I knew her, she was Gin's childminder and I liked her; she'd lived in London and she always had stories to tell. Once, when Gin wasn't listening, she'd told me she didn't see why I should marry someone I didn't know. She had her slippers on and a pink chiffon scarf which was covering a head full of rollers. I expected she'd be angry about having her evening disrupted but from the one shamefaced glance I shot her I could tell she was concerned.

'Check the pill bottle, it should be in the bathroom. I'll put the kettle on,' said Ginda. Eileen was quite lame. She hauled herself up the stairs laboriously and by the time she reappeared with the bottle – which was still about half full – Ginda was pouring me a cup of black coffee. She told me to keep standing up while I drank it. In the next hour or so she made me drink three cups of coffee and she and Eileen kept me moving round the living-room. It was well after midnight before they let me go to bed. As I headed for the stairs Ginda sighed and said, 'Nothing is going to change, Jas. Grow up and face facts.'

6

The best thing in my life at that time was Avtar. We'd stayed in touch and one Saturday I bumped into her while I was running an errand for Mum. We exchanged pleasantries for a bit, but then she suddenly dropped her voice and said very quietly, 'Are you having an arranged marriage?' I was so surprised that I dropped my guard; I looked right back at her and nodded. And she said, just as quietly, 'So am I.'

I saw her quite often after that. Avtar seemed to accept her marriage in a way I just couldn't. 'Mine's quite good-looking,' she shrugged. 'Anyway, Jas,' she gripped my arm and spoke through her giggles, 'I'm going to enjoy my life until I'm shipped off to India. You know that boy who lives in Violet Street . . . ?'

That was Avtar for you: happy-go-lucky, cheeky, much more daring than me. Her parents were just as strict as mine but sometimes, somehow, she slipped their control. She had three sisters and five brothers and the brothers guarded her honour all right. They gave her a really hard time when they heard that she'd walked home with a boy, or if she went out in a low-cut blouse. But they were busy with their own lives; as long as Avtar went about her business quietly she often got away with it.

If my mum had known this she would never have let me be friends with her, but she didn't so all she had to worry about was the fact that Avtar's family were a much lower caste than us. They were *chamar*. Mum had never let us have *chamar* friends. Years before I'd challenged her on that. I asked her why, if our *chamar* neighbour went to the same *gurdwara* as us, I wasn't allowed to play out with her kids. Mum beat me for that, but I never got an explanation.

I don't know why she condoned my friendship with Avtar. Perhaps it was because she had strict parents and protective brothers. But she did condone it, she even let me visit Avtar after school. I had to get permission to go; I had to say when I would be going and when I'd be back and, having said, I would never dare be even five minutes late. I wouldn't risk losing that freedom.

Avtar's parents both worked and all her brothers had jobs so we were often alone in her house. We'd watch TV programmes all through instead of quickly flipping channels if a couple started kissing like we always did in our house. We listened to music, secretly rifling through her brothers' record collections. We talked and talked.

One day we went into the living-room and one of her brothers was there, sprawled on the sofa balancing a cup of coffee on his chest. He didn't move at first, just looked at me so long and hard I felt myself start blushing. Then he swung his legs round, stood up and gave me a lazy smile.

'Hi, I'm Jassey. Make yourself at home, I'm just leaving,' he said.

Once he was gone Avtar looked at me. Her eyes were

stretched really wide and they were full of mischief as she burst out laughing. 'That's my good-looking brother. No need to ask what you thought of him: you should have seen your face!'

What happened next was really due to Avtar. She encouraged it: 'He was asking about you, Jas, I think he really likes you.' She engineered it: 'Look after Jas for me, will you, Jassey, while I make the tea.' She organized our meetings and acted as our alibi. But that came later; in those early days just being alone with Jassey while Avtar was in the kitchen felt like the most exciting thing I'd ever done. I'd never been alone with a male who wasn't Dad or Balbir. I'd never had a conversation with a boy, not even at school. But Jassey made it so easy; he was relaxed and friendly and he seemed interested in what I had to say. I felt we could talk for hours.

I started going round to Avtar's as often as I could. Mum and Dad knew where I was and they'd said I could go there, so I told myself that I wasn't deceiving them. I felt safe with Jassey. He was older than me, twenty-one when we met. He worked for an engineering firm in Derby but he was also a very keen boxer, semi-professional Avtar said. I surprised myself by telling him what I was going through at home and he surprised me by not laughing it off or telling me to accept it. He was a good listener and he was very sympathetic. I'd never before had anyone pay me so much attention.

As I was about to leave one evening about four weeks after we'd met he suddenly said, 'Will you go out with me?'

Without giving it a second's thought I said 'yes'. I could feel this big grin spreading over my face, and my cheeks flushed hot with pleasure. He looked pleased too, his face lit up. We were standing by the front door and he had his hand on the latch, barring my way.

'Avtar will tell you where to meet me,' he said, and then, leaning forward suddenly, he dropped a quick hot kiss on my lips. I was stunned; we stood there looking at each other for a second and then he swung the door open and gave me a gentle push, under the arch of his arm out onto the pavement. 'Bye then,' he said.

The next day Avtar was all giggles and innuendo. 'I'll call for you at six-thirty Friday,' she said. 'We'll pretend we're going round to mine but when we get to the top of my road Jassey will pick you up in his car.'

'But I'm at Presto Friday evenings.'

'Tell them you're not feeling well and you can't make it.'

'Mum will want to know where my money is.'

'You don't get much, do you? Jassey'll give it to you. He gets paid loads.'

She sounded so convinced I didn't argue. It was like I was in a bubble of excitement bouncing along at one remove from real life. When I was getting ready to go out on Friday Lucy came into our room and sat down on our bed.

'Why are you putting on make-up? You're only going to Presto.'

I pretended to be absorbed with my mascara and didn't answer.

'You're not going to Presto, are you? You've got your best trousers on. *And* that's your favourite blouse. Where are you going? What are you doing, Jas?'

I didn't even look round, but I could feel her gaze as she scrutinized my clothes.

'You're meeting someone, aren't you? I bet you are! Who is it?'

I'd finished doing my mascara. I put the brush down and turned to face her.

'Okay, you're right, I'm meeting someone. Just don't ask any more, okay?'

And she didn't. We both knew it was for the best. If you don't know, you can't get into trouble for not telling. If you don't know, when you're asked you can't say, even if they try to beat it out of you.

That first evening with Jassey was magical. It was just like Avtar said. She called for me. We set off for her house and at the top of her road there was Jassey waiting in a purple Escort. He'd rolled the passenger seat right back, so when I got in and lay back no one could see me. He knew to do that, I didn't have to ask him; in the Asian community lots of girls and boys have to hide their romance.

He drove for about fifteen minutes, right out of the Asian area and over to Markeaton Park, where I'd only been once or twice before, on family outings. We got out of the car and he put his arm round my shoulders and we walked away from the paths and through a wooded bit where the greenish-grey light coming through the leaves made everything look mysterious. I shivered and Jassey pulled me closer to him. There were so few people about that we could hear the racket the birds made as they settled in the trees. The ground was wet and our feet left silvery trails in the grass. I felt so full of happiness that I could hardly breathe.

On the way back we stopped at the children's play area and Jassey pushed me on the swings, higher and higher until, through my laughter, I was shouting at him to stop. He waited for the swing to slow down a bit, then he grabbed the chains and pulled it to a halt and, while I was still sitting there catching my breath, he nipped round the front and bending right down he kissed me, this time properly. I thought I was going to melt.

I had to be home at 10 p.m. We'd agreed I'd walk back by myself from Jassey's road because it wasn't safe for him to come anywhere near my house. I'd been worrying what I'd tell Mum about my wages, but Avtar must have talked to him because just before we said goodbye he dug in his pockets and counted out £6.25. 'There, that should keep your mum happy.' Then, very quickly because we were back in the Asian area, he cupped my face with both his hands and kissed me goodnight.

That was the first of several visits to Markeaton Park that summer. It was our favourite place to go because we felt safe there, away from the eyes of the Asian community. In Markeaton Park Jassey first said 'I love you' and I said 'I love you too'. I don't know if I meant it. I certainly wasn't thinking 'I want to spend the rest of my life with this man and have his babies', but I didn't want to stop seeing him. I wanted to be with him more than anything at that moment. I was fifteen and I had a boyfriend and in the hours I spent with him I could forget about my duty and my family's honour and my future with the man whose picture leered down from our mantelpiece. I think those times with Jassey are the closest I have ever come to carefree.

I was so happy I got careless. There is a pond in the middle of Markeaton Park which, at its narrowest point, has stepping stones right across it. One evening just around dusk Jassey set out to cross them. He rolled his jeans up to his knees and stepped out very slowly and carefully with his arms outstretched for balance. When he got to the middle he swivelled round on the stone he was on and called to me to join him.

I was laughing as I stood at the brink, but I took my first step and shrieked when I felt how mossy and slippery it was.

'Come on, I dare you. It's easy,' Jassey said, holding out an arm for encouragement.

I took the first three at snail's pace, feeling about for a sure footing before shifting my weight. But when I reached the fourth stone I stretched out to reach Jassey and that was that.

Splash!

The water wasn't so very cold, but it was murky and full of weed. I came up with green slime trickling down my face. Jassey was laughing and so was I, laughing and struggling to keep my balance as I splashed water at him. It wasn't until I'd squelched my way to the side and Jassey pulled me out that it dawned on me.

'If Mum sees me like this she'll find out about us.'

My hair was dripping and my clothes were plastered to me. Looking down at the muddy puddle forming on the grass beneath me, I was caught between laughter and tears. Jassey was struggling to keep a straight face as he pulled a piece of weed out of my hair.

'Here, take your top off and put this on.' He was holding out his jumper.

'I can't, I'll never be able to explain that.'

'You'll just have to run in quick and hope no one sees you.'

'Look at the time, we're going to be late, Jassey. Quick, we can't stay here any longer.'

That night he dropped me closer to home than usual. It was taking a risk, but I couldn't walk too far through the streets dripping wet. I bolted down Dale Road until I got to our house. Away from Jassey I didn't see anything funny in my situation and I could feel my heart bumping in my chest. Very gingerly I tried the front door handle, praying it wouldn't squeak. If it was locked I was really sunk; thank God it wasn't. Holding my breath I eased the door open and slipped inside, ducking down so I couldn't be seen through the frosted glass panel in our inner door. I could hear the telly in the living-room. Prayed that Mum was watching it. I leant back against the wall, plucking up my courage to take the next step. The stairs were just opposite the door and I decided to make a run for them. Three, two, one, I did it. I didn't even bother to shut the door behind me.

'Is that you, Jasvinder?' Mum's voice reached me as I hit the first step.

'Yes, Mum. I need the toilet,' I called back, taking the stairs two at a time. I rushed into the bathroom, locked the door, tore off my clothes and turned the bath taps on. I felt weak with relief.

7

It was inevitable that Mum would find out about Jassey but I never dreamt it would be me that told her. I did it because I was desperate and I couldn't think of any other way to save myself. It was on a Saturday afternoon and some of my aunties had come round for a visit. 'My daughter will get the tea for us, won't you, Jasvinder? She makes excellent tea, I feel confident that she is going to be a very good wife. Remember to use plenty of fennel, Jasvinder,' Mum said.

She was all puffed up and important as I passed the tray round the group of gossiping women, moving carefully between my elders and betters, smiling and respectful, eyes downcast as I'd been taught.

'Jasvinder will be going to Germany to make her marriage soon. A very good match has been made. We are pleased,' Mum said, fetching the photograph from the mantelpiece and placing it in greedy, outstretched hands. It was dog-eared now that so many of my aunties had fingered it, twisting it this way and that as they assessed my catch. 'Look how nicely he smiles, Jasvinder,' my auntie Dhanna said. 'Not long now and you will be smiling for him too.'

Soon. Mum had said soon; but how soon? When? I wanted to scream out 'I won't do it. You can't make me. I won't go.' But I didn't. I sat there as expected, impassive, dutiful and quiet.

My mind was in turmoil. The holidays were only days away and that made me very nervous. Every year a couple of Asian girls would disappear from Littleover during the holidays. It was easier if they went then, when the teachers weren't expecting them, weren't making accusatory 'absent' marks in the big black register each day.

'Four saris in her chest. Such an expense, but now there is only Lucy left for me to think about.' Mum was showing off. For years she had felt herself pitied and patronized: 'Seven daughters? Oh my, Jagir, what a fate!' But this afternoon she was the queen, surrounded by admiring courtiers, all nodding their appreciation at her cleverness in marrying off six girls.

I had a vision of myself clinging to my bed, refusing to leave the house. Then the ghost of a whisper came back to me, something I'd overheard Robina discussing with a friend. I only caught snatches: '. . . sleeping pills . . . carried onto the plane . . . woke up in a taxi . . .' but I knew what they meant. I felt a prickle of sweat forming on my upper lip. Mum wouldn't dare to drug me. Surely Dad wouldn't let them do that.

'Yes, Ginda has a daughter but also a son, Sukdev, we call him David. And Yasmin already has two fine boys and Prakash, you know, my daughter in London . . .' Mum was in her element. I'd never before heard her sounding so proud – or so fond – of us. I think that's what made me tell her. Either that or I had lost my wits through fear.

I waited until the aunties had gone and then, on my best behaviour, I carried the tea things through to the kitchen and washed them all up. When everything was put away I went to where Mum was dozing in the living-room and touched her gently on the shoulder.

'Mum?'

Behind her glasses she blinked herself awake.

'Mum. You know my marriage? Well, the thing is this. I can't go through with it.'

Mum was wide awake now, sitting bolt upright in her chair.

'You see it's like this, Mum.' I swallowed hard. 'I can't go away. I've got a boyfriend. I'm seeing someone here.'

Why did I do it? What was I thinking? Did I, even for a second, imagine Mum would say, 'Oh, fine. Stay here and marry an untouchable whose family means nothing to us.'

The effect on her was instantaneous. Grabbing my arm she pulled herself off the sofa-bed and started yelling even before she'd found her feet. She took a couple of swipes at me but then changed tack and started beating herself, tearing at her hair and clothes. She was calling out for Dad, for Ginda and Yasmin, for anyone who would listen. Robina, Lucy and Dad came running.

'Oh, the shame! What is this girl doing to me? She will kill me.' She clutched at her heart and steadied herself against a chair. 'All my life I have struggled to bring up seven daughters – seven daughters – and this one will not rest until she sees me dead. Ayee! I can hear them now, talking in the *gurdwara*.' She covered her ears and bent her head against the imagined gossip. 'Have you heard this now, Chanan? My daughter, *my daughter*, has a boyfriend. You have ruined yourself, girl. What will become of you? What will become of me? You have brought dishonour on us all.'

She went on and on until, having spent all her energy, she collapsed back onto the sofa-bed. I had sunk to my knees, sobbing, at the beginning of her onslaught but now, thinking to

make my escape while she was exhausted, I stood up and slowly
– very slowly – began to edge towards the door. Her hair had
fallen from her bun and it was hanging wild about her face, but
she spotted me and was on her feet again in seconds. She grabbed
me by the hair on the back of my head, thrust her face into mine
and screamed, 'You will stay in your room. Go there now. Don't
think of coming out. I should never have trusted you. You will
not go anywhere on your own.

'Chanan!' She jerked her head to indicate that Dad should
follow me and, raising a shaking hand, mimed the turning of a
key in a lock.

Dad followed me up the stairs. I was emotionally drained,
almost too tired to speak, but as we reached the bedroom door I
tried one last entreaty. I didn't quite dare to lean against him,
but I yearned towards him as I said, 'Dad, please, don't let her
make me marry him.'

He stood there looking sadly at me, then he gave a weary sigh
and, dropping his eyes so he didn't have to see the plea in mine,
he shook his head. I heard the key turn in the lock as I flung
myself face down on my bed.

For the next three days that room was my prison. The first
evening I was in there I heard Dad screwing a bolt onto the
outside of the door. If I wanted to go to the toilet I had to shout
out and whoever came to open the door would stand outside the
bathroom. Lucy brought me food a couple of times a day but she
never said much. She was angry with me and I knew why. I'd
heard Mum shouting at her: 'Who is he? Where did she meet
him? Don't try to protect that prostitute.' 'They've been to see
Avtar,' she said on the second evening. She'd brought me up a
bowl of dhal but the way she thrust it at me made it clear she
wasn't planning to stop for a chat.

'What did she . . . ?'

'Nothing.' Her hand on the door handle, Lucy cut me off. 'But Mum told her parents that she wasn't welcome here anyway. She said Avtar was to stay away from you and so were her brothers.'

'Did they . . . ?' Lucy closed the door on my question. I wanted to know if they had beaten Avtar. I hadn't thought about her until that moment. I'd barely thought of Jassey. My head ached from crying and my brain felt numb. In all the hours I'd lain on my bed I'd been tormented by a vision of me and the man in the photograph sitting side by side on a settee while Mum lectured us about honour. In my mind's eye my face was bruised and there were tears pouring down my cheeks.

I was so absorbed by this image that at first I didn't register the rattle on the window. When it came again I looked up and was quick enough to see a trickle of tiny stones slide down the glass. Two steps and I was there looking out. If I peered right round to the left I could see the street and there was Jassey's Escort right opposite the house. How did he dare? Where was he?

Suddenly the driver door opened and Jassey climbed out and walked along the pavement to stand beneath the lamppost just down from our house. He waved and my heart lurched at the sight of his slow familiar smile. Standing in the dim street light he started acting out a little charade. I tucked myself in behind the flimsy curtain and watched. His arms encircled the air in front of him and he planted a kiss on the imaginary person he was hugging. He pointed up to me and then down into the empty space in front of him. He tilted his head towards me and, with a clenched fist, bumped out the rhythm of his heart. If I ever really loved Jassey I think it was at that moment.

Then his mime changed. He pointed up to me, then to himself and then made out he was running. Given that his left hand was held out beside him, clenching thin air, I reckoned that I was supposed to be running with him. My smile faded as slowly it dawned on me what he was suggesting. Involuntarily I turned to look back into my bedroom, my *own* bedroom, a privilege my older sisters' marriages had bestowed on me. The curtain caught on my shoulder and the light from the street flooded in, illuminating the Magnum poster that I'd fixed above my bed with Blu-tack.

For a moment I stood there surveying the silhouettes of everything in that room that was familiar to me. The tangle of clothes that never quite got put away. The jumble of make-up spilling out across the chest of drawers. The narrow bed with its lumpy mattress and candlewick bedspread, mine alone and a haven after all those years of bed being a battlefield of arms and legs. The street light lit up the flowery wallpaper, the flowery carpet. I thought about how pleased and proud Mum was when we got them, 'the very latest design'. This was my bedroom and in all the time I had spent dreading my arranged marriage I had never actually envisaged leaving it.

I turned back to the street where Jassey, head on one side, was looking at me quizzically. I smiled and shrugged my shoulders. It seemed impossible. Where would we go? What we would do? Who would I be without my family?

Those were the questions that ran through my mind in the days that followed. On the third day, after Mum had given me a long lecture about doing my duty, the bedroom door was left unlocked, but not the front and back doors. I wasn't allowed to use the phone and I wasn't allowed out of the house unless someone was with me. I spent hours sitting by the window, wondering about my future and waiting for Jassey to drive past. He kept coming. It wasn't always safe for him to stop but he'd drive past slowly enough to clock that I was watching. I began to think he was the only person in the world that cared about me.

The Saturday after I'd first been locked up, Mum said I was to come into town with her and Robina. Everyone was out and she didn't want me alone in the house. I thought I'd relish being out and about but it felt humiliating being sandwiched between my mum and my sister, walking at their pace, not being allowed to stop when I wanted to.

They had a couple of things to buy, and as we made our way up the street I became aware of a strange person shadowing us. At first I wasn't sure if it was a man or a woman. It was wearing women's clothes but the hair was obviously a wig and the lipstick, well, whoever applied it must have had their eyes shut.

My first instinct was to nudge Robina and have a giggle, but something stopped me. We got to Bacon's where she was planning to buy some shoes and, while she and Mum discussed styles, they both relaxed their watch on me. That's when the person brushed against me. She – or he, I still hadn't decided – pretended they were moving towards the racks of shoes; they passed too close and I twitched away. I thought I felt a hand touch mine. A couple of seconds later it happened again but this time I moved so I could see the person's face.

It was Jassey!

My mouth dropped open in astonishment and I was about to say something but he frowned and shook his head almost imperceptibly. Again I felt the nudging hand but this time I met it and my fingers closed on a folded piece of paper which I quickly tucked into my pocket. Mum and Robina seemed to spend hours choosing shoes after that, then Mum wanted some spices and Robina needed something at the chemist. The shopping trip seemed to drag on for ever.

Eventually we got home and, with the note burning a hole in my pocket, I went straight upstairs to the bedroom.

I want to help you. We could go away together. I will look after you. Look out for me at 11 tonight J xxx

That's what the note said. I sat there for ages looking at it. I heard Mum rattling pots and pans in the kitchen. Somewhere downstairs Lucy and Robina were having an argument. Dad came in from the pub and turned on the telly. If I went, would it finally make them understand?

I had to talk to Jassey but that seemed impossible when there was always someone watching me. Suddenly it struck me that there was a way to buy back my freedom. I considered it for a couple of seconds and then stood up and went downstairs.

I stopped in the kitchen doorway. Mum was at the stove.

'Mum, I've changed my mind, I will get married.'

She whipped round. Her face was stern but her voice was gentle as she said, 'What did you say, child?'

'I will get married, I will go through with it. I'll do it for you and Dad.'

'Good. At last you've come to your senses,' she said, nodding approvingly. As she turned again to her cooking pot I thought I saw a change in her bearing, her shoulders seemed to relax.

My announcement worked just as anticipated. The front and back doors were still locked but I wasn't so closely watched. The atmosphere changed. People were pleased with me, aunties who had lectured me came round and patted me and pinched my cheek. I forced myself to smile. Mum hummed as she smoothed and refolded the fabrics in my chest. The air was sticky with the smell of sweets, dozens of them being baked for me to take with me to my new relations. Their cloying scent hit the fear still settled on my stomach and made me nauseous.

My freedom was still very limited. I lived for the moments when I could ring Jassey. He never dared ring me. Our conversations were brief and urgent. I was scared. Mum hadn't said anything about dates but I could tell from the way preparations were going that they would be sending me away any day. I overheard her on the phone discussing flights to Frankfurt for me, her and Ginda. I couldn't think straight but Jassey seemed so confident.

'You can't marry a stranger,' he said. 'I'll look after you. We'll be fine.'

We made plans. I hid a small suitcase under my bed and gradually I packed it. I had to be careful no one noticed what went missing. All I took was a few clothes, a photograph of my dad and a photograph of Ginda's eldest, David, because I loved him very much. At the last minute I put in a panda bear that Robina had made at school in needlework. She'd given it to me several birthdays back and now it had a half-torn ear and an eye hanging off, but it was precious to me.

We'd worked out how to get the case out of the house. I couldn't just carry it out the front door because even if Mum and Dad didn't see me, one of the nosy neighbours in our terrace would. The night we'd agreed to do it I stayed awake until 2 a.m. I was so worn out with worry it was hard for me. I kept dropping off then jerking back awake. When the time came I tiptoed along to the bathroom, keeping as close as possible to the walls so the floorboards didn't creak. I'd pulled the sheet off my bed and now I knotted it really tightly to the handle of the case. My heart was beating so hard I could almost hear it.

I flushed the toilet to disguise the noise of the sash window scraping open then I ran the tap as, standing on the seat, I gingerly lowered the case down into the garden. The sheet wasn't quite long enough and I suffered agonies of indecision before deciding I would have to let it drop. It landed with a dull thud. My mouth was dry and the blood was pounding in my ears. I stood there frozen as I waited to hear Mum stamping out of her bedroom, come to see what was happening. A couple of minutes passed and nothing broke the silence. I sank down onto the toilet seat and sat there with my head in my hands until my pulse slowed down.

Next morning I woke with a start at eight o'clock. Mum would have gone to work and I could hear Dad in the bathroom. I hurried downstairs, through the shed and into the garden. The case was gone. Having checked no one was watching from an upstairs window I looked behind the stack of empty seed trays piled up by the back gate. My sheet was there, neatly folded. As I picked it up I felt the crackle of a piece of paper beneath the top fold. It was a scrap torn from a paper bag.

3 a.m. WE DID IT! J xxx

8

I spent the next few days in limbo feeling as if all my drive and energy had been sapped. I was ready to go but I couldn't imagine going. This was my home. It was what I knew and who I was. I looked in the mirror and fancied that I saw myself dissolving.

Then something happened to snap me out of my torpor. I was woken one morning by the sound of the front door slamming. I looked at my watch: it was late. Mum would have been at work for hours, Dad would be asleep after his night shift; it must have been Lucy going out. From where I lay I could hear her footsteps hurrying down the pavement. Something – instinct, intuition, call it what you like – made me want to see if she had remembered to lock the door behind her. Perhaps it was just hope. I climbed out of bed, went downstairs and gingerly tried the handle. The door opened. I closed it again instantly, and as quietly as I could. I knew I had to seize this opportunity.

Upstairs, I tore a page out of one of my school exercise books and sat down to write Mum and Dad a note. There were so many thoughts crashing round inside my head that I struggled to find the words to describe why I was going, how I felt. I kept crossing bits out and starting again: I wrote three or four versions but in the end what I left on my pillow was this.

Dear Mum and Dad,

When you read this I will have gone but I can't say where. I've tried to explain things to you but you won't listen so I can't stay here any more. I'm too young to get married. I want to go to college and make you proud of me. I want to have a life.

Don't worry about me because I'm going to be okay. I love you both very much and hope I will see you again soon.

Your loving daughter, Jasvinder.

Once it was done I wanted to go straight away. I had nothing to pack. I told myself to wait a while. Jassey was at work and he didn't know I was coming. It would be better to wait until the working day was over, but I was terrified that Lucy would come back. I sat down in front of the telly and tried to concentrate but I found myself looking at my watch every five minutes. I drank two cups of coffee. The house seemed deathly quiet. Even the street outside seemed dead and empty. At about twelve o'clock I couldn't stand it any longer. I got up and ran.

I ran as if the hounds of hell were after me, up Dale Road, Normanton Road, into the centre of town and out again. I was so scared of getting caught, it was not until I was well clear of the Asian area that I slowed my pace a bit; I was hot and I needed to catch my breath.

With only the vaguest idea where Jassey's workplace was I got lost several times but I wasn't bothered. Outside the Asian area I felt anonymous. When I asked directions I was careful to ask white people and I was glad to see I didn't spark their interest, they barely noticed me. Eventually I found the engineering works, tucked under a bridge on the outskirts of Derby. There were a good two hours to go before Jassey's shift was over, so I sat down on a wall to wait for him. I sat there willing the hours to pass. My heart was racing, but time seemed to have slowed to a crawl, eking out each minute between the ending of my old life and the beginning of my new one.

Jassey was absolutely shocked when he came out and found me there. I was too caught up in my own feelings to give him credit for that and I babbled on, oblivious to his incomprehension. When I paused for breath he said, 'We can't go now. We're not ready.'

'But we've got to go. Don't you understand? I might not be able to get out of the house again.'

He stood there, twisting his overalls in his hands, looking really worried.

'But Jas, what about work? I haven't told them. I can't just . . .'

'You said you'd help me. You said you loved me. Well, now's the time. I'm telling you Jassey, it's not safe for me to stay here any longer.'

He came round quite quickly although it can't have been easy for him. His workmates were streaming past, calling out and teasing him for talking to me. Once he'd made his mind up he said he'd need about an hour to go back to his house, pack his stuff and get mine. He said I was to stay there and wait for him.

That was the longest hour. The sun went in and as the streets emptied I felt conspicuous and cold. Eventually the purple Escort pulled up beside me. Jassey was looking hassled but he managed a smile. His mum had seen him carrying cases out of the house and asked where he was going. 'I just told her I'd be back later.' He hadn't even had time to leave a note for her. At that moment

I was too self-absorbed to think what that must have meant to him.

My heart was racing. It was six o'clock: Mum would be getting home soon and people would realize I was missing. Then they'd start looking for me. I was scrunched up in my seat, trying to see out of the car window without being seen myself.

'Where are we going to go then?' Jassey said.

I gawped at him. We'd never even thought about that. He picked a map book off the back seat and opened it at the page with Derby on it. 'Here,' he said. 'Close your eyes and point. Wherever your finger lands, that's where we'll go.'

So I did. My finger landed on Newcastle. It meant nothing to me; I'd never been; I didn't know anybody there. Jassey said he'd been once, to visit an auntie, years before. It took us about four hours to drive there and we hardly talked at all. What I had done was beginning to sink in, and my stomach was churning with a mixture of relief and terror. The fact that I had actually managed to escape made me feel elated, but at the same time I was convinced that at any moment someone would catch up with us and drag me home again. Just outside Derby a police car passed us with its siren screaming and I sank down into the footwell of my seat and remained crouched there for the rest of the journey.

Jassey was scared too, and very worried about what we'd done. During all our preparations I don't think he'd really considered things properly. I was so young, so naive, although I don't think he saw me like that. He never took advantage of me, or made me do anything I didn't want to do. As far as he was concerned, he'd fallen in love with me and I was in trouble and he wanted to help.

It might sound very romantic but Jassey and I were not

Romeo and Juliet. I wanted to teach Mum a lesson. I wanted her to say, 'Oh, all right then, come home, you don't have to get married. Finish school. Go to college. Do all the stuff the other kids are doing.' I must have been mad.

We stopped once on the way and got a cup of tea and some chips, and it was after ten o'clock by the time we reached Newcastle. We'd agreed that we'd sleep in the car to save money until we could find a room to rent, so Jassey found a public car park and we pulled our jackets over us and tried to get comfortable. I can remember biting really hard on my collar so that Jassey wouldn't hear me crying but he did anyway, and for what felt like ages he sat up, stroking my hair.

The next morning I woke up feeling cold and stiff, with all my worries sitting like a rock on my stomach. It felt so strange not having to watch the clock; I'd been used to having every minute monitored, now time stretched ahead of me like a vast blank canvas. We washed our faces in the public toilet in the middle of the car park and got some more tea in a café and then tried to sort ourselves out. We needed somewhere to stay and a job for Jassey, so we trailed up and down the streets looking at the ads in newsagent windows.

Finally we just sat in the car. We were so scared of being seen. Although I kept telling myself I was really glad I'd escaped, I couldn't help imagining what it would be like if I was still at home. I blanked out the chest full of bridal fabrics and that picture on the mantelpiece and just saw me and Lucy watching telly in the living-room, Mum in the kitchen chopping vegetables for the curry, and Dad sitting opposite her at the kitchen table sipping his tea before the night shift. It was all so warm and familiar it made me ache with longing. I grabbed hold of Jassey's hand and squeezed it really tight.

We were desperate to save our money, but living in the car was so grim that after a couple of days we checked into the Heron Hotel. A really lovely old couple ran it. They invited us to watch telly with them in their lounge and gave us tea and biscuits and they asked us so many questions – not prying, just friendly – that we ended up telling them our story. After that they let us stop another night without paying.

It must have been on about day four that we came across a shopkeeper who said he had a place that we could stay in. It was very dingy: one room three floors above his shop, with a shared kitchen and bathroom one flight down.

There were cigarette burns in the carpet and the only furniture apart from the bed was a chest of drawers and two hard chairs. The bed looked quite clean but the mattress was really thin. The kitchen stank of old grease, only one ring worked on the cooker and there was a pane missing in the bathroom window so it was permanently freezing. I felt my stomach lurch as Jassey said we'd take it. Home, in comparison, was a five-star hotel.

I thought that often in the months that followed, months when it got so cold that we could make jelly and leave it on the windowsill to set overnight. I was from a working-class family, no doubt about that, but until Jassey and I moved to Newcastle I'd never felt poor. At home we'd always had hot water and clean clothes and enough to eat. Now, especially in the weeks when Jassey couldn't get much work, we often only ate one meal a day; sometimes we couldn't afford anything more than a bag of chips. I got used to bathing in the lukewarm trickle of water that the decrepit Ascot boiler spat out, but there was never enough of it to wash our clothes so we used to save up our fifty-pence pieces and take them to the launderette every two or three weeks. I'd brought very few clothes with me and those I had soon looked worn and grey but there was no money for anything new. I was beyond caring about my appearance anyway, and for the first weeks, before I felt confident enough to go out and start looking for work, I never went anywhere that it mattered what I looked like. The area we were living in was rough. The all-seeing eye of 'the community' used to drive me mad in Derby but at least I never feared coming to physical harm on the streets. In our squalid area of Newcastle even Jassey's old Escort was a target for thieves and it was broken into twice. I never walked outside alone at night.

We tried to keep ourselves to ourselves and avoid the Asian areas but even so Jassey managed to pick up snippets of information; there was talk about us on the Asian grapevine. He learnt that my mum and dad had been round to his place and demanded to know where I was. Avtar was beaten until she finally persuaded her parents that she didn't know anything about our whereabouts. When I heard this I was glad we hadn't told anybody or implicated any of our siblings in our 'crime'. For years that's how I saw our escape; I felt I was the baddy and my family were the goodies and that didn't feel nice.

We heard a rumour that my mum and dad had hired a private detective and about ten days after our flight from Derby the police caught up with us. Early in the morning – before Jassey had set off on his daily search for work – there was a knock on the door. It was such a strong, authoritative rat-tat-tat that we guessed at once that it was the police. I was sitting on the bed and Jassey gestured that I should stay there as he went to open the door.

'Jaswant Rattu?'

From my position out of sight of the door, I could see Jassey nodding his head.

'I have reason to believe that you have abducted and are now harbouring a young lady, Jasvinder Kaur Kang. She went missing from her home in Derby ten days ago and has not contacted her family since. They are very concerned for her safety. Can I come in so we could discuss this?'

As Jassey stood back to let the policeman cross the threshold, I rushed forward, tears pouring down my face, and blocked his way.

'It's not like that.' I scrubbed at my tears with my sleeve. 'Jassey didn't abduct me, he rescued me, I asked him to take me, he was trying to help me because my parents are trying to force me into a marriage, he's never hurt me, it's them who . . .'

'Slow down, Miss, slow down and then we can get this sorted out. Now, if you wouldn't mind me coming in?'

I drew back to stand beside Jassey and as the policeman stepped inside I saw him run an appraising eye around our dingy room with its unmade bed. Our bed. I wanted to hide that from him. What we did together there was so beautiful and magical and mind-blowing that I couldn't stand to have it held up for scrutiny.

The policeman was tall and heavily built. He took off his helmet and I could see that his hair was greying and he had a fatherly air about him.

'May I?' He gestured to one of our two chairs. Jassey took the other and I sat back down on the bed.

'Now, if you'd like to tell me the whole story, but go slowly please so I can get it straight.'

So I did, I told him everything, starting with the fact that the plane ticket had been bought and how if Jassey hadn't rescued me – I made out he was the saviour in the whole situation – I would have been forced to go to Germany to get married. I explained that I didn't want to get married, let alone to someone I didn't know, because I wanted to finish school and go to college. I told him that Mum and Dad wouldn't listen to me no matter how much I begged them to, and I even told him about Prakash and Ginda and how their husbands beat them. Then I swore blind that Jassey hadn't put me up to anything I hadn't wanted to do and pointed out that I'd be sixteen in just a few weeks.

All the time I was talking the policeman sat there listening; occasionally he looked surprised or nodded his head. He was so quiet and kind and it was such a relief to pour it all out.

'I've seen this before,' he said, when finally I'd finished. 'I understand your position, Miss, and I understand why you did what you did, so don't worry: I'm not going to tell your parents where you are. What I will do is tell them that you've contacted the police and that you are safe. And I think it would be a good idea, Miss, if some time soon you would ring them and tell them that yourself. All right then?' He gave an encouraging smile. 'Good luck to you both,' he said, as he stood up and left.

I wish I could remember that man's name because I owe him a debt of gratitude. If he'd taken me home I'm sure I would have been on the next plane out to Germany and the rest of my life would have turned out very differently.

9

I longed to make that call home but for weeks I didn't have the courage. Time – acres of empty, unmonitored time – stretched out, leaving Derby further and further behind, and I yearned to do something that would close the gap. It was the comfortable familiarity of it all that I missed. I wanted to walk down our street and know the people that I saw; I wanted to go into our corner shop and put my hand on the groceries on my list without having to think twice; I wanted to stand in the playground at Littleover, laughing with my friends. If you'd told me the previous term that I'd mind leaving school I'd have laughed, but . . . I kept thinking of the English teacher who'd handed back my essay saying, 'Very good, Jasvinder. You're showing promise.' What good was promise now?

Images of home teased me, dancing in and out of my mind. I'd see Mum sitting on the floor in the living-room peeling onions. Dad standing on the back doorstep, his hand cupped around a cigarette. I can't believe I'm writing this, but I almost missed Mum's nagging: 'A bag of flour and a white loaf and straight back, mind, no loitering or skipping off.' In those days she always knew where I was.

I knew I'd call home eventually and in my mind I ran through the conversation I'd be having many times: Mum answering the phone, calling across to Dad, 'It's Jasvinder. She's safe!' Everybody crying, telling me I was forgiven and that everything was going to be all right.

I couldn't have been more wrong.

Mum's harsh words cut me to the quick – even today I wince at the sharp pain their memory brings – but almost as bad was the fact that she didn't even ask where I was. She hung up on me without even trying to find that out. It was like she was already being as good as her word:

'In our eyes you're dead.'

Deep down inside I couldn't really believe Mum had meant that. I couldn't accept I meant so little to her. I wrote to her, hoping words could bridge the gulf that had opened up between us.

Dear Mum and Dad,

I hope you are well. I am well but I miss you very much. I wish I could see you, or even talk to you. I think of you a lot.

I'm sorry I made you cross by running away and I hope you can forgive me, but you know why I left. I didn't want to leave you, but I didn't want to marry that man either. I'm too young to get married. My teacher at school said I could do A levels. I want to make something of my life.

Please forgive me, I'd like to come home. I miss you very much. I love you both and I wish I could be with you. I hope I will be, some day soon. Please tell my nephew David that I love him.

Your loving daughter, Jasvinder.

I sent that letter and then I kept ringing, more and more often, but every time it was the same. If Mum or Dad answered, they'd just put the phone down. I felt I'd been kicked every time Dad did that.

Once I rang and Lucy hissed, 'Do you realize what you've done to us? How difficult it is for Gin at her house? Do you know what they're saying in the *gurdwara*, that people spit at Mum in the street?' And then she hung up.

I'd thought my sisters would support me but I was wrong. I don't know if the things they said were true. All I knew was that my whole family was rejecting me and they were saying this is *your* fault; this is because of what *you've* done.

Poor Jassey. When I could force myself to focus on our situation, it looked impossibly bleak. There we were in a strange city, cut off from all the people we knew and loved. Jassey had given up his secure job and income for my sake, and there didn't seem much work to be had in Newcastle, not for Asian people anyway. He'd been my knight in shining armour; he'd done it because he loved me, and that made me feel bad too, because although I loved his kindness and his sweet funny ways, in my heart of hearts I knew I'd never really loved him.

I'd made my bed and I had to lie in it. We had somewhere to live. Once we'd signed on for benefits we found somewhere a bit nicer, somewhere that was clean at least, but we still didn't feel settled. When I turned sixteen I started to look for work, but my heart wasn't really in it; most days I just sat on our bed wrapped up in my thoughts. With every day that passed I got more and more depressed. I'd lost my dad, my mum, my sisters, my brother, my nephews, my nieces, all those aunties who had so annoyed me with their busybody ways, my friends, Avtar . . . everybody. The only reminder I had of home was my two photographs and Robina's little cloth panda. I used to cry myself to sleep and I would wake up crying in the morning and the panda would be drenched with tears. My cheeks were red and raw. My skin flared up with all the anxiety and in the afternoons when Jassey came home we used to trawl the health shops looking for herbal remedies. Sometimes my homesickness and guilt and fear and loneliness would chase each other round my mind so furiously that I felt possessed. I'd peer into the mirror trying to see if the turmoil inside me was visible on my face. Sometimes I didn't recognize the blank face of the person staring back at me. I felt so isolated I didn't know who I was any more.

When it got really bad, Jassey put me in the car at five in the morning and drove me down to Derby just so I could see and smell the place where I'd grown up. He drove past my house then parked a small distance away so I could see my dad walking home from work. I watched him trudge along, his thermos and his newspaper – the Asian paper, he never learnt to read English – tucked under one arm. His feet dragged slightly and my heart bled. He looked much older than I remembered. I had to stop myself leaping out and chasing after him; once I gripped the edge of my seat so hard I broke my nails. I longed to talk to him but I knew if Mum found out she'd be furious and I didn't want to get him into trouble.

Sometimes we parked outside Dale primary school where my nephews and nieces then went and I pressed myself against the playground fence and watched them with their friends. I reached my hands out as if to touch them. It comforted me to see them looking so carefree. At least *they* weren't old enough to hate me.

Those visits were a bit like watching a soppy movie. For a couple of hours I could step out of my reality and pretend I was part of someone else's. Sometimes, driving through those streets

I had known all my life, I could almost feel happy; the look of relief on Jassey's face when that happened made me realize what a burden he was carrying. He was endlessly supportive. But I was always crying again before we got back to Newcastle. My family had washed their hands of me, they were completely out of my reach, but I couldn't stop loving them.

It didn't help that Jassey was back in touch with his family. He waited a few weeks, until we were sure that they weren't going to send anybody after us, and then he rang home. His mum was really pleased to hear from him, she said she'd been worried sick about what my family might do to him. She wanted to know if he'd got work and where he was living, if I was cooking for him properly. I don't think she asked anything else about me, but she accepted our situation and she didn't blame Jassey for what he'd done, not on the phone at least. After the first few months we even saw them sometimes and the fact that he still had his family rubbed salt in the wound left where mine had severed our connection. He was still their son but I was no one's daughter.

'What does that make me? Who am I?' I used to wail to Jassey.

'You're my sweetheart,' he'd say, and hold me close. I leant on him so heavily during that first year in Newcastle. He bore the brunt of all my moods and feelings. Sometimes I had good days but the slightest thing – even the thought of my nephew's birthday – would lay me so low that I couldn't face the world outside our door.

It was to cheer me up that Jassey first suggested we drive to Whitley Bay. It was a Saturday morning four or five months after we'd run away and I was sitting on our bed, too apathetic even to get dressed. Normally Jassey would have tried to coax me out of my mood, clowning around until he made me smile, but that morning he simply said, 'Come on, get up, we're going to the seaside.'

I'd never been before. It was less than an hour's drive from our flat. Jassey kept singing a Cliff Richard song, 'We're All Going on a Summer Holiday', and it did feel a bit like we were going on holiday. For the first time in months we were having a break from the grind of trying to build our life together.

We found a car park and walked past the amusement arcade to get to the beach. I will never forget my first sight of it, ever. I stood there on the promenade looking at this vast expanse of sand and beyond it sea, sea, sea right out to the horizon and I just thought 'Wow'. I couldn't believe that I had lived in England all my life and never before seen this extraordinary phenomenon. There was so much more of it than I had ever considered possible. I stood there and I could feel the boundaries of my world expanding: if this exists, I thought, what else is there I haven't seen?

Jassey grabbed my hand and pulled me down onto the beach. The silvery sand felt so heavy underfoot; I sank a bit with every step and it poured over the edges of my shoes. I stooped to pick up handfuls of the stuff and found it was nothing, it just flowed through my fingers and was gone, caught in the wind and carried off to infinity.

'Let's paddle,' said Jassey, who was already rolling his jeans up. We kicked off our shoes and socks and raced down to the water's edge. The dry sand scratched and crunched between my toes, but when we crossed the scummy line marking the retreating tide, I was astonished to find it transformed into a hard, cold surface. Holding hands and laughing we stood on the brink and then shrieked as a wave rolled in, soaking our trouser legs.

'It's freezing,' I yelled, dancing in the foam. We dodged the waves until our toes went numb and then, collecting our shoes, started walking down the beach towards the lighthouse at the end of it. It was a beautiful day, cold, but the sun was bright and for the first time in months we behaved like the young lovers we were supposed to be. Jassey flicked some seaweed at me and I screamed and ran away but then as I pulled the slimy strands out of my hair I saw all the little bubbles it was made of and discovered you could pop them. We skirted the water's edge trying to stay just far in enough to stop the waves swallowing our footprints. We hopped as far as we could, kidding ourselves that anyone who came after us would think they were following one-legged people. We found a sharp-edged stone and used it to write our names in the sand. We wrote, so big that all the world could see: 'I love you Jas', and 'I love you Jassey' and a heart with an arrow through it.

Eventually we came to a rocky outcrop near the lighthouse and, moving carefully on our cold, bare feet, found a smooth bit to sit on. For a while we were quiet, looking out across the sea, its iron-grey surface corrugated by white-fringed ripples. The seagulls screeched as they swooped and dived, and I gave myself up to the smell and the sound and the feel of the wind whipping over us. But Jassey was never quiet for long. Standing up, he gave an elaborate bow and said very solemnly:

'You are my sweetheart and I love you so much and to show you just how much I am going to drink sea water out of your shoe.'

He picked up my shoe, dipped it into a nearby rock pool and did as he had promised. At least he took one gulp and swallowed but then he gagged and spluttered and used the excuse of giving another bow to spill the rest. I laughed and laughed and as he came and sat beside me, folding his arms around me, I realized that, for the first time since we'd left home, I felt really happy.

Eventually we walked back along the beach and bought fish and chips and sat on a wall eating them. It wasn't until I was full and contented, licking the vinegar off my fingers, that I realized that in all the time we'd been at Whitley Bay I'd never once thought about Mum, Dad or my sisters. It struck me as strange then that I didn't know if Mum and Dad had ever seen the sea, except from the ship that brought them over. I could imagine Dad enjoying himself here, standing with his hands in his trouser pockets, smoking a cigarette and looking out to the horizon, but I'm not sure Mum would have liked it.

I wrote about that day in our diary. It was something we'd decided to keep together; Jassey said that one day we'd give it to our children. We were supposed to take it in turns to write but Jassey never seemed to find the time and I teased him about it. I wrote:

It's me again because he's too lazy to write our diary. Today my sweet took me to the seaside and told me he loved me and drank sea water out of my shoe.

Then a couple of days later Jassey picked it up and wrote:

Sweet is nagging me again to write in this book. What she doesn't understand is that I work to feed her and clothe her and she has such a big appetite. But I love her dearly, she is my life.

10

We must have stayed in Newcastle about twelve months but that time is a blur to me. My days were long and purposeless and they all seemed the same. We never felt settled; I never stopped feeling like a fugitive. We were scared to tell the truth about who we were and what we were doing so it was hard to make friends. We felt so far from Derby, the city where our hearts were stranded. I felt that most keenly at holiday times. During *Diwali* I thought my heart would break. We were irresistibly drawn to the Asian area where we belonged. The pavements were clustered with people out visiting and parading their new clothes. Candles flickered in the windows of all the houses round us. At home Mum used to put candles in every room, even our bedroom, and for that one night it would be like living in a twinkling fairyland. She'd cook samosas and their hot, spicy smell would fill the house as she dropped them one after another into the bubbling oil. She let us eat loads.

Those memories were so vivid and so painful. *Diwali* is a special family time, and Jassey and I were on our own, hundreds of miles from home. We were lonely and, without our families, we were lost. That was the same for both of us. We'd been brought up by strict controlling parents who directed our lives and supported us along the routes they'd chosen for us. On our own we were rudderless. Until we ran away we'd always done what was expected of us; torn from that expectation we were aimless and uncertain. We were drifting on a frightening and uncharted sea of possibility.

One problem was that Jassey couldn't find regular work. Engineering was what he knew and there were engineering works in Newcastle but they didn't seem keen to employ anybody Asian. He did what he could get so we could survive – factory work, waiting, security – but he longed for something better.

That longing took us to Leeds. I don't know why we chose Leeds, it could have been London, or Huddersfield, or Manchester. Anywhere really. We just felt that if we moved on things might fall into place. We sold Jassey's Escort to raise some money and in its place we bought an ancient Toyota which was good on fuel. Having piled it high with our worldly possessions we set off. Leaving Newcastle didn't mean any more to me than leaving the bedsit in which I'd spent day after miserable day, week after week. I never, ever thought I'd miss it; I'd spent so long considering that dingy room to be my prison but it was a palace compared to the first place we found in Leeds.

We were back at square one, traipsing up and down scruffy streets scouring each newsagent's window for a card advertising a room we could afford. We had so little money and we couldn't claim benefits without an address so on the first day Jassey accepted a place that, under any other circumstances, I wouldn't choose to house a dog in.

The man who showed it to us, with his great beer belly

hanging over his trousers, behaved as if he was showing us the Hilton. Then he flicked the ash from his cigarette onto the floor, and when I watched him use the toe of his shoe to grind it in I understood how the carpet had come to look so grimy. You could hardly see the pattern on it and it felt sticky underfoot. The whole place smelt: a mixture of stale cigarettes and something I felt sure was urine.

We were too embarrassed to inspect the bed closely until we had handed over a week's rent in exchange for the key, but as soon as our new landlord shut the door behind him we raced over to it. It was infested. When you pulled back the greying bedcover you could see the creepy crawlies with the naked eye.

'We won't get in, we'll sleep on top of it,' said Jassey, quickly jerking back the cover so the horrible things were out of sight. 'In fact, you can sleep on top of me, then you won't have to touch it.'

That's what we tried to do. If it hadn't been so grim, it would have been funny. We got ready for bed by putting on our coats then Jassey lay flat on his back and I lay down on top of him. The fact that we managed to fall asleep like that shows how tired we were but, of course, I kept rolling off Jassey onto the filthy mattress and climbing back on again woke us both up. In the morning we were exhausted and Jassey was covered in bites that had him scratching like a monkey.

We were out of there by half past seven. Our rent included use of a kitchen but one peep round its door was enough to persuade us we didn't want to go in any further. From where we stood we could see mouse-droppings all over the counter. Just round the corner from our room was a greasy spoon café where Jassey said we could have breakfast. Its door was shut against the cool morning air and the windows were all steamed up on the inside.

We pushed our way in and were immediately enveloped by a fug of comforting smells: beans and toast and frying bacon. Jassey ordered two mugs of tea and one plate of toast to share.

'But I'm hungry, can't we have a fry-up?'

'We can't afford it, sweet, you know that. We've only got forty pounds to last us until I can find work or we can pick up our benefits.'

'All I know is that you're always saying we can't afford things. If we're hungry we should eat. You're just tight-fisted, that's your trouble.' My stomach had started to rumble at the sight of laden plates of eggs and bacon being whisked past our table and it was making me bad-tempered. Jassey looked so crestfallen that I immediately felt guilty and ashamed. I leant across the table and kissed him.

'I'm sorry, sweet, I didn't mean it. I know you are trying to make things work for us and I'm grateful, I really am. Maybe Leeds is going to be a better place for us.'

We lingered over those mugs of tea as long as possible. We were determined not to spend a second longer than we had to in our filthy, grotty room and the day stretched ahead of us, long and empty. Our priority was finding somewhere decent to live and by lunchtime we must have read every single 'To Let' card in ten newsagents' windows. I felt as if I'd been trudging up and down the network of narrow streets for ever and still there was nothing in our price range, nothing we could even ask about.

We needed a break to lift our flagging spirits and Jassey suggested we go and look at Roundhay Park. We thought we'd walk round it but when we got there we just threw ourselves down on the grass and lay there side by side holding hands. For a while we watched the white clouds scudding through the brilliant blue sky above us but gradually the warmth of the spring sunshine soothed us to sleep. It was gone four o'clock by the time I woke up again. Jassey was still fast asleep and I tickled his nose with a blade of grass until he jerked awake sneezing. The sun had gone in and I felt slightly damp and cold but my mood was definitely lighter.

Roundhay Park became an oasis to us in the next few days. We went there every afternoon when our search for somewhere to live became too depressing and we'd spin out the hours wandering through its many acres. We walked for miles; there were woods carpeted with bluebells, the ruins of the old castle to explore and Waterloo lake where we sat and watched the swans and herons. One day when we've got money, I told myself, I'll come back here with bread and feed them.

On about the fifth day we sat on a bench quite near the entrance and shared a take-away burger for our lunch. When we'd finished Jassey got up to get rid of the greasy wrapping and there, right at the top of the bin, was a copy of that day's *Yorkshire Post*, which someone had dumped. He fished it out and while he was reading the news, I opened the classifieds and began browsing the flats to let section. I wasn't expecting to find anything we could afford, I was only doing it to pass the time, but one particular flat jumped out at me. I nudged Jassey.

'Listen to this, this sounds great.' I marked the ad with my finger and started reading. 'Two bed flat with verandah, Round-hay. Separate lounge. Kitchen. Bathroom. £30 per week.'

I turned to Jassey expectantly but he didn't even look up from the page he was reading. 'Forget it,' he said. 'We can't afford it. It's way out of our price range.'

'But can't we just go and look? It's somewhere near here; just where we want to be. They don't know we can't afford it, and anyway there's nothing to stop us looking. It would give us something to do.' I jumped up and started trying to drag Jassey to his feet. 'Come on, sweet, please. It'd be better than sitting here all afternoon.' Jassey sighed and smiled at me; it hadn't been difficult to persuade him.

We found a phone box; Jassey rang the number in the ad and arranged for us to go round at four o'clock that afternoon. The address was Newton Court, Roundhay. We drove over there in good time and found it easily. The flat was one of four in a big white house with an open verandah which led off the kitchen and ran round the front of the building. Someone had put chairs out so you could sit overlooking the garden.

The door was opened by a young man, about the same age as Jassey. He introduced himself as Anil. He had thick slicked-back hair and flashy clothes and we later found out he was half-Asian, half-Iranian. He was really friendly as he showed us the flat and it was gorgeous. There wasn't much furniture but the lounge had a settee and a small round table and chairs to sit on and, although one room only had a mattress on the floor, the bed in the bigger bedroom looked newish. The whole place was fresh and clean and I loved it. We had a look round and then he offered us a cup of tea and explained that he was in the import business; dealing mostly in fabrics but sometimes carpets. He and Jassey were getting on really well; for so long we'd had no one but ourselves to talk to. I could hear Jassey telling him about us leaving Derby and wanting to make a home for ourselves, but I couldn't concentrate on the conversation because my whole mind was thinking, 'Somehow we've got to live here.'

Eventually Anil said, 'So, what do you think of the place? Do you want to take it?'

Normally I would have let Jassey do the talking but this time I butted in immediately. 'It's nice but it's a bit expensive. Is there any chance that you might drop the rent a bit?'

He looked really surprised. It could have been partly because I'd been so forward; up until that point I hadn't really said much. He thought for a bit and then he said, 'Look, like I told you, I'm in the import business and I'm away a lot but I need a room in Leeds sometimes, maybe four or five nights a month. If you don't mind me using that second bedroom when I need it we could call it twenty-five pounds a week. How would that suit you?' Jassey and I just sat there, grinning like idiots.

That flat brought me back to life a bit. It wasn't in an Asian area and that felt liberating. When I thought about it, I realized that it was a long time since we'd felt the need to lose ourselves in a crowd or be invisible. The rumours Jassey heard about people trying to track us down when we were first in Newcastle had dried up months and months ago, which was a relief, obviously. But it hurt having to accept that my family didn't even care enough to look for me.

Still, having a decent place to live made all the difference and I began to feel some energy flowing back into me. I started cooking meals for us and it made me feel like I had a bit of control over my life. I cooked Asian food because the taste and smell of it was always comforting. I liked the line of spice jars on the wall by the cooker. We got on really well with the owner of the flat and it felt – for the first time since we'd run away – as if we weren't completely isolated. Work was still a problem though and Jassey signed on for benefits.

I was still calling home regularly at that point. I never stopped craving any tiny crumb of contact. I know now how hard you have to stamp on hope before you can crush it altogether. The calls became almost formulaic. Lucy answered after two or three rings and her 'hello' was pleased and welcoming, as though she was expecting a call from a friend. When she heard it was me she muttered something disappointed or exasperated like, 'Oh it's you,' or, 'Won't you ever learn' before ramming the phone back on the hook. Mum and Dad took longer to answer. I used to imagine Mum heaving herself off the floor and walking heavily towards the phone. They never said anything in greeting, just waited silently for me to announce myself. I'd know if it was Mum because she put the phone down really quickly, but if it was Dad it took longer, and sometimes before the click I'd hear a heavy sigh. The one thing I regretted about having our own phone was being stuck in the same room with it when the line to my family went dead. At least when I was calling from a phone box I could walk away, distance myself from the rejection and clear my head.

One night something different happened. Lucy answered and she didn't hang up. I was so surprised I faltered.

'Lucy? Is that you? Have I got the right number?'

'I can't talk now, call back tomorrow morning,' was all she said.

I was in a fever of anticipation. It was almost two years since I had spoken to anyone in my family, I'd had no contact and no news. If anything terrible had happened would it have reached me on the Asian grapevine? I hoped and believed so but I had no way of being sure and now I was terrified that Lucy had only agreed to talk to me so she could break bad news. I rang again about half past nine next morning. My heart was racing but Lucy sounded calm.

'How have you been?' she said as though we'd been chatting only a month ago.

'Yeah, fine. How are you? How's Mum and Dad?'

'They're all right. Where are you living then?'

'In a flat, in Leeds.' It was so good to hear her talk without criticism in her voice that tears were running down my cheeks and splashing on my jumper. She didn't ask much more about us, but she answered my questions. David, my little nephew, he was fine. Yasmin had given birth to a boy, and so had Robina, but she was back home because her marriage hadn't worked out. Lucy sounded quite matter-of-fact about that, but I was horrified. Poor Robina! She must have been so unhappy and I wasn't even there for her. 'How is she?' I asked but Lucy had moved on, she was telling me about Prakash, who was a widow now since Bila died of drink. Then, suddenly, she said, 'There's someone at the door, I've got to go,' and before I could say anything else she put the phone down.

I sat there for ages going over our conversation in my mind. Lucy's manner made it clear that it was all old news, but to me it was like being hit with a cannon ball of information. So much had happened I needed time to sort it all out. My main thoughts were with Robina and I was trying to get straight what Lucy said. It was something about Navtej not coming to Britain but moving on to Canada and marrying someone else. But what about his baby? My fingers itched to dial the number again but I didn't dare to. I didn't want to risk upsetting her. Having been in isolation for so long, having any news at all meant so much to me and I was just so grateful for it. I felt like my family had been dead and were now brought back to life again. I decided I'd wait to see if Lucy would speak to me again in a couple of weeks.

For the first six months in Leeds Jassey did casual jobs here and there and then we decided to try and make a go of a market stall.

We'd spent long enough mooching round markets killing time and Jassey always liked the atmosphere, the hustle and bustle, the constant change and challenge. He liked the easygoing, good humour of the stallholders too and we became quite friendly with a couple of them. They encouraged us to try it.

Jassey was always a wizard with money and now he managed, somehow, to save and scrape together £50 to get us started. He found out where the warehouses were and what they had to offer and we invested in small, battery-operated goods, things like watches, torches and alarm clocks. It cost £5 a day to take a pitch in Kirkgate market and at first we just did Fridays and Saturdays.

We watched the other stallholders carefully and learnt all their tricks, like how to make £20 worth of stock look like a million dollars. We used to drape an expensive-looking bit of cloth over the stall and then cover it with boxes. It didn't matter if the boxes were empty, they were just there to make it look as if your stall was laden. Then you put your best bits and pieces at the back, because it meant that to see them properly people had to lean right into the stall to see what was what. Once you got them doing that you were halfway to selling something.

I began to realize that right at the start when people approached the stall, they wanted to be left alone. If you made the first move too soon you frightened them off, so I'd always pretend to be busy, re-arranging stuff or chatting to my neighbour. It wasn't until a customer actually touched something that I'd engage with them. I might say something about the different styles available, or I'd tell them about any special features, luminous hands on a watch for instance. If they showed interest in any one thing for more than a few seconds I'd begin to put the pressure on. I'd tell them that particular thing had been selling like hot cakes all morning and I only had two of them left, even if I still had hundreds piled up beneath the stall. Or I'd say that, since it was the last one, they could have it for a knock-down price. We'd buy digital watches for 25 pence and sell them for £1.50; on a Saturday you could sell 100 of them. It was easy.

I found I had a natural gift for selling. I surprised myself by how good I was, and I liked the human contact. All the time we were in Newcastle Jassey had been my only link with the outside world and I'd felt frozen inside. Now in the hurly-burly of the markets I began to thaw out. There were people to say hello to when you arrived to set up, stamping your feet and banging your hands together against the morning chill. Customers became familiar and they'd stop to chat. There was always someone to have a laugh and a cup of tea with. There was life and I felt I was on the fringes of it, plucking up the courage to jump in.

For the first time since leaving Derby I thought Jassey and I might make something of our life together. We made a good team and we soon started doing the indoor market at Kirkgate as well as the outdoor markets. By the time we were working regularly several days a week we had stopped worrying about having enough money to eat properly and begun to set ourselves targets: we bought ourselves a take-away meal, we went out for a drink, we took out hire purchase on a television.

My family's rejection of me had made me feel totally worthless but now I found I could do something, and the day we brought our television home I felt so elated I really wanted to share that with them. I kidded myself that my parents would be pleased for us; certainly Dad would. If only Dad would answer the phone, I thought, everything would be all right.

I was determined to ring and tell them my news before they hung up on me. I planned exactly what I was going to say and when I'd dialled the number and the phone started ringing I took a deep breath in readiness.

It was Mum who answered but, after a second's hesitation, I plunged in anyway.

'It's me, Mum. It's going well for us, we've got a market stall and we've saved enough to . . .'

The line went dead before I got the sentence out. I'd long since lost count of how many times that had happened, but it still knocked me back. My face felt hot, flooded with shame, hurt and humiliation. That's when I understood that my success would never please them. As far as they were concerned I was an outcast and outcasts belong in the gutter. 'Without us you'll end up in the streets,' is what Mum had threatened when I first called home and now I saw that was what she wanted. The thought that I could survive – let alone thrive – outside the protective, prohibitive scaffolding that had encased her and Dad all their lives was anathema to them. I should have understood that.

11

We stayed in Leeds almost a year and then, out of the blue, Anil announced that he was selling the flat and moving away from the city. It was a blow but by that time Jassey had set his heart and mind on building a business and he wanted more space to store all our stock. He decided we should branch out in Bradford, not much more than twenty minutes' drive away.

Our new address was White's View, Bradford. It was a second-floor flat in a row of back-to-back houses, on a narrow street which ran all the way up a steep hill. I'd never before seen anything like those houses. They were built so close together that there was no room for any gardens at the back, and at the front it looked as if they were all tied to one another with a cat's cradle. Those were the washing lines, bits of string running between the upstairs windows and fixed to a pulley so that all the women could easily hang their washing out or bring it in again. I found the sight of them quite cosy, but I couldn't help thinking that Mum wouldn't have approved of the arrangement. She wouldn't have wanted strangers seeing Dad's vests, let alone her bits and pieces!

The fact that I could think about Mum in an almost light-hearted way shows the frame of mind I was in when we first arrived in Bradford. The year in Leeds had been good for us and I was feeling much stronger, less reliant on Jassey carrying me through each day. White's View changed that. The flat was small and poky and it was infested with mice, but those weren't the things that mattered. The problem was that White's View was right in the heart of the Asian area and I hadn't banked on what being back in that situation would do to me.

'Are you new here?' said an elderly woman standing beside me as I queued to pay for milk in the shop at the end of our road.

Before I had time to think, years of Mum's discipline rose up in me and, keeping my eyes respectfully on the ground, I answered, 'Yes, Auntie-ji. I've been here one week.'

'Where have you come from?'

'Leeds,' I murmured.

'Is that where your parents live?' she asked. Silence fell and transactions ceased as the shopkeeper and his customers tuned in to my answer. Unabashed by my reluctance, unembarrassed by her own directness, my inquisitor pressed on until she found out my family's whereabouts, my father's name and that of the village he had come from in the Punjab.

'I have an uncle in the Punjab,' she said, turning her back on me at last to buy her milk.

Everywhere I went in my new surroundings it was the same: questions from strangers who wanted to place me and possess me and suck me into the vortex that swirls around any place where Asians congregate. The questing, inquisitive undercurrents that had tugged at me throughout my childhood were every bit as forceful here in Bradford. I was scared their greedy embrace would reach back to Derby and discover the truth about us, so I started telling lies about my parents. As the lies multiplied I struggled to remember what I'd said to whom; and once again I became uncertain who I was.

All my life I'd hated the suffocating feeling that comes from being constantly watched and judged and now, in a city of curious strangers, it grew stronger. But even as I shrank from scrutiny my heart twisted with envy as homesickness took hold again. Each morning I would stand at our bedroom window looking down on the groups of head-scarfed women going about their business – sisters, daughters, mothers, aunties, nieces – and I would ache with loneliness.

It set me right back. I could feel myself slipping towards the dismal days in Newcastle when, I would say in retrospect, I was suffering from depression. In those days I was in and out of GP surgeries with backaches and headaches and skin complaints but if anyone ever asked me how I was feeling in myself I said 'fine'. That's what I'd been taught to do. Physical ailments were one thing, no shame in that, but your state of mind was something you kept firmly to yourself.

If I'd been going to tell the truth at any time during those long, miserable months, I'd have said my mind was like a quagmire. All Jassey's efforts to cheer me drowned in its murky depths. I was still convinced I was the one who had done something wrong and sinned against my family. Guilt hung over me like a big black cloud. Because of me people were spitting at my mum in the street. She was a battle-axe but she was who I'd grown up with, what I knew, and the thought that I'd brought shame on her made my guts shrivel. I felt really small.

The truth was I needed her. I'd been challenging Mum since right back when I was tiny but when I won, when I escaped and got my freedom, I didn't know what to do with it. She and my sisters were the only role models I'd ever had; I didn't know how to lead a life outside the confines of the community that had always cocooned me. Being in White's View reminded me of that. I was surrounded by women leading the life that I'd rejected. Standing alone at my window, watching their busy, bustling lives, I sometimes wondered why.

Two years before in Newcastle, with Jassey doing odd-jobs and me stuck in our bedsit measuring each day in empty, endless hours, I'd had no answer. Now, thanks to our market stalls, I'd found a purpose. All the hard work we'd done in Leeds had driven depression's black dog from my shoulder, and now in Bradford the need to keep working kept me from brooding and stopped me sliding backwards. Jassey and I had built a business. We'd started with nothing but determination and the stamina to work long hours and we'd made something successful.

We were so successful by the time we got to Bradford that Jassey decided he could run the markets single-handed. His next target for us was to buy a house and he said we needed a second income; he wanted me to get a job. He was still the one making all the decisions, so I went along with it. I got a job in Argos. It was nothing exciting, not as much fun as working in the market, but I accepted it because Jassey said it would help to build our future. And on cold wet days I was glad to be inside.

It was not long after we moved to Bradford that Jassey's parents first visited us. While we were in Leeds Jassey had popped back to see them every now and again and although I was happy for him, the injustice in the different ways our families treated us rankled. His family were totally accepting of our situation. They were kind to me and welcoming. They teased me about being their *jatti-nor*, which means their higher caste daughter-in-law, and although there was no malice in it, it stung because I knew most of Mum's problem with Jassey was his being *chamar*. I found it a strain putting on a show of happiness, and I used to be glad when their visits were over.

It was some small consolation that I was talking quite regularly to Lucy by then. Our conversations were usually brief, but at least I had news of my family. She told me when her marriage was arranged. She'd been promised to the man I stood up; it was a face-saving arrangement but she didn't seem to mind. She sounded so grown-up.

Having that little bit of contact made me crave more; I plucked up the courage to ask Lucy if she would meet me somewhere and, to my amazement, she agreed. She said I should come to Derby and I suggested Markeaton Park, our old hiding place. She said she would meet us there on Saturday afternoon.

She was waiting in the car park and my heart leapt when I saw her. I jumped out of the car and hugged her so tight that eventually she pushed me off. It was only then that I took in her appearance. She'd been hovering on the edge of adolescence when I left Derby, still proud of her long, thick plait, hoping Mum wouldn't hear if she played kiss-chase in the playground, happy to wear her Indian suits at home. Now she was wearing a really fashionable western skirt and a fitted blouse and she'd had her hair cut, in a short, sleek bob. I was amazed that Mum had let her out of the house dressed like that. And I soon found out that her appearance was just the start of it.

She climbed into the car with us – we weren't bothered about being seen any more but she didn't want to get caught with us – and started telling us about her life. She seemed much more confident than I'd remembered. While she was waiting for her marriage to happen she had so much freedom. She was allowed to go out with friends, she was going to the pub, she was even going to nightclubs. She was doing things that I and my other sisters had never even dreamt of. I should have been happy for her, but I was shattered. I'd had to give up my whole life – my family, my friends, my education, everything – for the sake of my freedom and now it seemed Lucy had been handed hers on a plate. I felt it made a mockery of everything I'd been through. I sat beside her on the back seat of the car nodding and smiling but all the time she was talking I was thinking 'I should have stayed, I needn't have done this'.

But there was no going back. Lucy made it clear that, as far as Mum and Dad were concerned, I wouldn't be welcome. She was adamant that she didn't want to discuss it and I didn't want to spoil the time I had with her by pushing it, so an awful lot of what was on my mind got left unsaid. She spent about an hour with us and then she got out of the car and went back to the world that used to be mine. What little peace of mind I had went with her.

Later, back in the flat, I talked it through with Jassey. As always he was calm and sensible.

'It's *because* you ran away that Lucy has that freedom. Don't you see, your mum must be terrified she'll lose another daughter.' A corner of my rational mind knew that must be true, that I must have paved the way for her, but it was swamped by a swirling mass of guilt, regret and misery.

'Could I have compromised?'

'Might things have changed anyway?'

'If I'd stayed, could I have had a proper life?'

Those were the thoughts that chased each other round my mind until I longed to force my fists through my skull and batter them into silence.

*   *   *

I went on seeing Lucy. She came to Bradford too, looking stunning in high heels and a red suit with a fish-tail skirt. She'd cropped her hair and had it dyed; I felt so drab in comparison. The first time she visited I felt uncomfortable as I watched her running her eyes around our tiny flat. I thought she must be thinking, 'Well, you've got what you deserve,' but she didn't say anything. On her second visit she brought Robina with her and Sunny, my nephew. He was about three and you could see Robina doted on him. When she looked at him her eyes were so full of pride and love that she seemed radiant despite all she'd been through.

She had so much to tell me. It was a beautiful bright day and we put Sunny in his pushchair and wheeled him over to our local park. It was time for his rest and he lay there, sucking on his dummy, while we sat on a bench and Robina talked and talked until she'd told me everything. I felt as close to her that afternoon as I had been when we were at school together.

At last I got the full story of her marriage breakdown. She'd never managed to get Navtej into England. They left Germany and went to try their luck in Canada where Navtej had family. But things hadn't worked out as they hoped so she came home. There was no need for a divorce because their ceremony in India had sealed the arranged marriage without being legally binding. She'd arrived back in Derby more than a year ago.

'Mum and Dad have been very good about it, they let me come home, and that's where we've been living. It's been nice having the support with Sunny, it's right for him to be near his family, his real aunties, Ginda-*masi*, Yasmin-*masi*, all the cousins.' There wasn't a trace of self-pity in her voice, she sounded quite happy with her life, and I soon found out why.

'I've met someone else, Jas, and he's asked me to marry him.'

'You *met* him? It's not arranged then? *Robina!* What do Mum and Dad think?'

'They're all right, they've accepted it.' She was looking down into her lap just like a blushing bride but I think she was embarrassed about what she had to say to me. 'He's a *jatt* like us, Jas, he's from a good family. They're happy for me, they're even going to pay for the wedding.'

I was dumbfounded. Mum and Dad happy about a *love match*? Had they changed completely? Why were things so much easier for my sisters than they'd been for me? The child in me wanted to shout out, 'That's not *fair!*' but I controlled myself. I managed to say, 'So when's the wedding going to be then?'

'We're not sure yet. He's in prison at the moment.' She looked up and smiled reassuringly at me. 'It was nothing serious. But he's coming out at the end of next month and then we'll fix it.'

She was busy with her wedding preparations and then with her new husband so in the next few months it was Lucy I was most in contact with. She told me about Robina's wedding when it happened. They'd done the whole thing: there was a big ceremony, they poured oil on the doorstep of Mum and Dad's house before Robina went back into it, all the women had cried when they said goodbye to her. It was a proper Sikh wedding and all the family were there, except me. Even Robina had made it clear she didn't want me there.

It was Lucy too who told me when Dad got ill. He developed jaundice and was taken into hospital. I kept fretting about what could have caused it. 'The doctors say all the worry and stress hasn't helped him. Mum says he's been getting old and sick from the moment you ran away,' said Lucy, shrugging her shoulders.

He was in the hospital for weeks and I used to lie awake at

night wondering and worrying about him, asking myself if his illness really was my fault. 'Why don't you go and see him?' said Jassey. By then he was driving down to Derby quite regularly to see his family and I could easily have gone with him. I did go once, but we got as far as the hospital car park and I lost my nerve. How would I react if Dad was hostile towards me? What would I do if Mum was already in there with him? I sat there for an hour with the flowers I'd bought him wilting in my lap. In the end I didn't see him. I couldn't do it; I just wasn't brave enough.

12

When I was eighteen I fell pregnant. I was taking the pill but it happened anyway. I was still so naive that I didn't recognize the signs; I'd gone to the doctor because I felt so tired and sick and he confirmed it for me. 'Not married?' Dr Bazu was writing notes and his turban obscured his face but I could imagine the look of disapproval, hear the tut-tutting he would later do with his wife.

'Where was it you said your parents were living?'

'I didn't, but it's not near here.' The appointment was drawing to a close and I stood up quickly. 'Thanks for your time,' I said and left without giving him the chance to pry any further.

Jassey was thrilled. When I told him he went running round the room, jumping in the air like a little kid. For the whole of that evening his face was one big cheesy grin; I don't think I'd ever seen him look so happy. Before I told him I hadn't known what to think. Cut off from my family, creating a family of my own seemed inconceivable, but Jassey wasn't having any of that.

'You'll marry me now, won't you, sweet?' He was down on

one knee, holding my hand. 'Our baby is going to need a respectable mum and dad; we'll be a proper family and I will look after you both.'

It was what he'd always wanted; he'd asked me to marry him several times before and now I had a strong feeling that I owed it to him. He was a good, kind man with my best interests at heart and I knew he would never hurt me. Besides, what was the alternative? I felt, ironically, as if this was my arranged marriage and I had to make it work. I also believed that if I had any chance of redeeming myself in my family's eyes it would be by becoming respectable. If I had a successful husband, a baby and a nice house, perhaps they would like me again. They might even have me back.

Robina helped me prepare for the wedding. I guess she thought she'd get away with it as long as she kept her involvement secret from Mum and Dad. All my life she had been my role model, and now she stepped in to play the part of mother. We went round all the shops together, looking for a wedding sari. There are so many Asian shops in Bradford it took hours, but Robina never stopped being light-hearted and merry. She was determined to make it a special day for me and it was special. For the first time in years someone from my family was playing a part in my life.

Robina was determined I shouldn't miss out on all the most important parts of the ritual, and she bought me a maroon wedding sari, embroidered with so much gold that it weighed a ton. When I first tried it on I couldn't believe anyone could wear it for more than half an hour.

Then, when the day came, she was there in time to dress me. She shooed Jassey out of the flat and sat me down in the bedroom so she could do my make-up. She plastered on foundation, followed by bright red lipstick and the *bindi* on my forehead. I hadn't worn make-up since I was fifteen and when I looked in the mirror it didn't feel like me at all.

She also covered me in golden jewellery. We couldn't afford to buy any, so she'd lent me hers: bracelets, necklaces and the special gold chain that runs round your head and across your face to your nose. She treated me exactly as my mum should have done and made me look every inch the Asian bride.

For a split second as I stood there in my fineries, I felt proud of my heritage: the lavish drama of my costume, all that gold honouring a tradition that stretched back down the centuries, the *bindi* denoting the caste of which Mum and Dad were so proud. But the feeling didn't last. Because I was an outcast it was all empty symbolism. I hadn't done the proper Asian thing so I couldn't have a proper Asian wedding. Robina was trying to make it all real for me, but inside I just felt terribly small and sad. I wasn't going to be shown off to hundreds of people; there wasn't going to be a big family gathering; I wasn't even going to be seen by my own mum and dad. My wedding was just an hour in a registry office with Lucy and Robina and Jassey's family. Afterwards we went back to the flat and ate some food that my sisters had made. No one stayed long. In their absence Mum and Dad took up more of the room than they ever would have done in person and it made us all feel awkward. Jassey and I were back at work the following day.

I went on working at Argos and helping Jassey in the markets until I was five months pregnant. By then Jassey was doing so well that we didn't have such a pressing need for money, and I was tired, weighed down by constant yearning for my mum. We'd never been close. I'd managed to survive three and a half years without even talking to her but now, with the baby growing inside me, my need for her was sharpened. I wanted her to pat my swollen belly, I wanted her to be there telling me to get enough rest and eat right, I wanted her to show me what it means to be a mum.

It was left to Jassey's mum to do that. Jassey was working so hard he had no time to look after me, so he sent me down to stay with her a month before my due date. We decided we wanted the baby born in Derby where we belonged.

I was fat and bovine by the time I got there. Jassey's mum was kind and solicitous and I was placid and passive, accepting her care. Avtar had married and was waiting for her husband to arrive from India. I had seen her several times in the years since we left Derby but the pert schoolgirl I'd known had been replaced by a respectable woman and we couldn't seem to find the friendship we'd once so enjoyed. Strangely, staying in Derby barely fifteen minutes' walk from Dale Road, I felt even more cut off from my family than I had in Bradford. I didn't even fantasize about creeping round to try and catch a glimpse of Dad as I might have done a few months back. Without the stimulus of work to bolster me, my thoughts began to spiral. I felt like I was going through the motions of a life I hadn't chosen. I was an outcast and I was having a baby; those were the facts and nothing I could do would change them.

Jassey made it down from Bradford in time to see Lisa born. I was glad to have him there to prove I was a respectable married woman, because I was much the youngest on the ward and the midwives scared me with their disapproving frowns. He held my hand and they gave me an epidural and the whole thing passed in a bit of a blur. His mum was the first one to come and see us. She patted my cheek and said, 'Never mind, dear, next time it will be a boy.'

To me it didn't matter. I loved Lisa from the second they placed her perfect, blood-streaked body in my arms. In those precious, shell-shocked moments after the birth Jassey stood there with his arms encircling me and this brand new life we had created and the tears poured down his face. 'Why would I want a son when I've got this beautiful creature?' he said, much later, after his mum had left.

Robina came to see me. She brought Sunny with her and the prettiest pink baby dress you've ever seen. Sunny was fascinated by Lisa. He sat on Robina's knee, holding the edge of the bassinette and blowing kisses to her.

'I've told Mum about the baby and I think she's going to come and see her. She said she might. I'll talk to her again when I get home.' Robina's face was all encouragement and enthusiasm but the reunion between me and Mum – although it did happen – wasn't what she'd hoped for.

She came the next day. I watched her walking down the ward towards me and my first thought was that in the years since I'd seen her she hadn't changed a bit. She was encased in a fur coat and her bearing was formidable, tall, stout and proud. Her lips were pursed and her face was stern and, short of going backwards, she couldn't have seemed more reluctant. Robina kept looking over her shoulder to make sure she was still following. When they finally reached me Robina indicated the chair by my bed, so Mum could sit right by me and see Lisa in her bassinette. Mum ignored that. She stood there, stiff as a post, clutching her bag close as if she was scared of touching something dirty.

'Hi, Mum,' I said. We'd never been a physical family but I was aching for her touch. I clenched my fingers round the sheets in an effort to control myself. 'This is Lisa.' As luck would have it my baby, Mum's grandchild, was wide awake. I'd put her in the pink dress Robina brought and smoothed the shock of black hair that she'd been born with and she was lying there, tiny and innocent with her brown unblinking gaze.

Mum glanced into the bassinette for as long as it took to ascertain there was a baby in there. Me she acknowledged with the curt nod she might give a little-known acquaintance in the *gurdwara*. Then, without having said a word, she turned her attention to the comings and goings in the rest of the ward. Robina tried valiantly to keep some sort of conversation going but we both knew it was impossible and long before the visiting hour was over she escorted Mum out. As I watched them walk back down the ward I thought my heart would break. The last time I spoke to Mum she said I was dead in her eyes and now she'd proved she meant it.

About two weeks after Lisa was born Jassey took me back to Bradford. I hadn't heard from Mum again. Her indifference had set me right back and if I hadn't had Lisa to look after I don't know what would have happened to me. She was an easy, sunny baby; in her first few weeks she slept a lot and made few demands. She started smiling and there were days when her gummy smile and the funny little cries she made were the only things that anchored me to life.

I don't know where the days went to. I kept the curtains drawn. If I looked outside the streets seemed to be filled with women moving in happy gaggles. I'd see a couple of head-scarfed sisters, backs bent in symmetry as they heaved their pushchairs up our hill. There was a group of young girls that used to pass by, all linked arms and swinging plaits. A girl about my age used to walk alongside while an older woman – I was sure it was her mother – carried her baby. They were forever leaning over to wrap the shawl a little closer round its tiny head. I felt like a freakish monster in my isolation.

Sometimes I couldn't find it in myself to get up all day and Lisa would happily lie there beside me on the bed. She'd grip one of my fingers with her tiny, determined little fist and her brown eyes would fix on my face, following my every move with fascination. During those long hours alone with her I thought a lot about mother love. The moment the midwife placed Lisa in my arms the depression that had been blanketing my emotions was pierced by something so fierce it was almost painful. I felt tremulous, proud, passionate, tender, fearful, joyous . . . Had Mum ever felt like that about me? I wondered. And if so, where had those feelings gone to? Had they died or were they hidden somewhere, stifled beneath her protective cloak of honour? As I nursed Lisa, cradling her fragile body close, I vowed I would never allow anything to dull my feelings for her.

Jassey would come home from work and find us lying there. Sometimes I'd still be in my pyjamas. He'd sweep Lisa up into his arms and demand to hear every detail of what we had been doing. He used to look after her while I had a bath or he would urge me to get dressed and we'd all go out and get some food in. I ate all day – comfort food I barely tasted – and the weight piled on, but despite my greed, I couldn't get to the shops without Jassey, even the corner shop which was no more than fifty steps from our front door. I was scared to go out alone; even when I was with him I kept my eyes on the ground and clung to his arm as if for protection. I'd lost all my confidence.

Was that hormonal? Was it post-natal depression that brought me so low? Nobody suggested it, but then I never gave them the opportunity to do so. I made the appointments that Lisa needed – vaccinations and so on – but when I saw the midwives I made sure I kept my feelings to myself. Perhaps professionals could have helped me. Medication might have numbed the pain but it couldn't change the glaring fact that my own mum had shut the door on me. Before her visit to the hospital I had hope. I'd left home an errant schoolgirl but now I was a married woman with a thriving business and a beautiful baby. Was there nothing she could find to like in that?

Once again, Jassey did his best for me. He was always trying to cheer me up; he'd pull funny faces at me to make me smile, he bought me flowers. It was he who suggested I take up aerobics when I complained about being so fat.

He understood how the loss of my family tormented me and, although we didn't talk about it any more – what else was there to say? – he did his best to fill the roles of mother, father and friend as well as husband. He tried to be all that he could to me. It wasn't his fault that it wasn't enough.

It makes me smile to remember the only thing he gave up on, teaching me to drive. He didn't want me straining to push Lisa up and down the hills of Bradford and so he started giving me lessons: 'Clutch, clutch,' he screamed as I hiccoughed my way up a hill. The car stalled and I jammed on the handbrake. 'Fine! You drive if you know so much about it,' I said, leaping out of my seat and slamming the driver's door behind me. I didn't look back as I stamped down the hill, but I could hear the line of cars behind him blaring their horns in anger.

Even that he forgave me. He drove round until he found me and then, right there on the pavement, he hugged me and told me that it didn't matter.

'You and Lisa are my pride and joy.' He was always saying that; he even wrote it in our diary.

He was my rock and my support and, if he could, he would

have carried me for ever. But as his business grew, so did the demands it made on him. He was leaving home at 4 a.m. to set up his stalls and sometimes, when he was collecting stock, he wasn't back before midnight. When he did get home early he'd shovel down his dinner and then start on his paperwork. He'd always been so quick with numbers, but now he seemed to find it hard. I'd hear him cursing when he couldn't make the figures add up right. Once I found him asleep with his head on the table and a screwed up piece of paper balled in one hand. He'd always been well-organized, but now he was forgetful, almost careless: he couldn't remember where he'd left his car keys, he got stranded on the motorway when his van ran out of petrol.

One evening when Lisa was about twelve months old he came back from work and, as he always did, came straight to find us. I was feeding Lisa in the kitchen. He kissed the top of my head, tickled Lisa's neck and then, as he put the kettle on, he said, 'You have to pull yourself together, sweet. There's too much for me to do now. I need your help.'

I looked up from spooning rice into Lisa's baby-bird mouth and I saw Jassey, really saw him, for the first time in weeks. It was a Sunday and he'd left for the market at 4 a.m. Now, under the harsh electric light, he looked exhausted. There were dark rings under his eyes and he needed a shave. His clothes were baggy on him and I realized, with a jolt of surprise, that he must have lost weight. The guilt that was always there, lapping at my conscience, rose up and flooded my face.

My friend Lizzie who I'd met at Kirkgate market became Lisa's childminder and Lisa settled with her very well. I went back to the markets and joined Jassey working seven days a week, moving between sites. With me back in the business he could take on twice as many stalls and we agreed that I should look after the outdoor markets in Leeds while he focused on sites in Morley and Bradford. It was two years since I'd set out a stall, but all the old tricks came back to me. The patter flowed easily, I recognized my regular customers and always had a friendly word for them, I never got the change muddled. I was a good saleswoman and rediscovering that seemed to spring-clean my mind. Work, as usual, was a panacea. Jassey and I were making a success of our business and contributing to that success boosted my spirits.

But as the deadening cloud of depression lifted I found myself staring into the face of an uncomfortable truth. Jassey was so busy working for our future that he didn't seem to register the cracks in our present, but to me they were growing ever wider. In the months following Lisa's birth the emotional closeness that had carried us through my darkest days began to dwindle. We still had fun together, but it was largely through Lisa. What little free time we had was devoted to her. We took her to the park and, taking one hand each, we'd swing her high into the air with her feet kicking up through the autumn leaves and her little voice shouting with laughter. We spent Sunday afternoons at the zoo and basked in the saucer-eyed wonderment with which she viewed the elephant. We took her swimming and were dizzy with pride when she splashed her plump sausage legs.

Those moments glued us together and beyond our mutual absorption in Lisa it was still true to say that I relied on Jassey and he looked after me, but more and more our relationship seemed to me like a business partnership. I felt I was trapped in the sort of empty marriage I had fled Derby to escape.

Jassey didn't notice because our life was working out just as he wanted it. We had a decent car and a van and, within eighteen months of Lisa's birth, we had bought our first house. It was on the outskirts of Bradford, away from the Asian area. In White's View I'd never got over the feeling of being watched and judged; each time I went out I imagined that people held their daughters close, not wanting them tainted by that shameless woman who disgraced her own family.

The house we bought was something to be proud of. It was semi-detached with a big garden and a garage with a bright red door; it even had a driveway. I remember the day we moved in Jassey carried Lisa round the house, showing her all the rooms, talking to her about the life we were going to lead there. I followed in their wake, keenly aware that the enthusiasm I should have felt was being drowned by guilt. Jassey had built for me the life that every Asian woman dreams of but deep down inside I didn't want it. For all we'd been through together, all I owed Jassey, I still couldn't love him. He'd worked so hard to buy me a home and now, try as I might, I couldn't drag my heart through its door.

13

I don't know what made Mum decide to start speaking to me but one day, out of the blue, she did. It was only her and Dad left at home by then. Robina was living in Leicester with her new husband, and Lucy had gone to Germany to join the man she'd been married to, so Mum no longer had to brandish her honour in front of them. My brother Balbir had gone too. He was living with Dawn, the half-white woman he'd taken up with before I left home. 'Mum's not happy with it, but she'd never say so,' Robina told me on the phone. 'She still rushes round after him when he goes home, still treats him like a king.' The injustice of this twisted my guts into tight knots of anger, but even then I couldn't quash my longing for acceptance. I went on ringing and one day Mum said, 'Hello.'

'Mum, is that you?' I said, determined to keep the wobble from my voice.

'Yes.'

'How are you?'

'All right.'

'How's Dad?'

'All right.'

'Has he gone to work?'

'Yes.'

'Have you been at work?'

'Yes.'

'Does my auntie . . .'

She cut me short – 'The doorbell's ringing. I have to go now' – and put the phone down.

We spoke quite often after that. It was always me that did the ringing, and all she ever said was 'yes', 'no', 'yes', with the occasional weary sigh in between. She never volunteered anything, never asked about me or Jassey or even her granddaughter, Lisa, but she was there at the other end of the line and she didn't hang up and she wasn't abusive. I was supposed to be grateful for that, it was supposed to be enough and in a funny way it was because I had no choice. For so long I'd had nothing and at least this was something, some tiny scrap of recognition that she was my mother. That's what I longed for. I wanted her to acknowledge that we belonged to one another, I wanted her to see that casting me out was wrong, I wanted, more than anything, to feel her affection. I wanted to be loved unconditionally like I loved Lisa.

It didn't happen. Those brief, staccato calls – moments of elation followed by hours lost in disappointment and regret – did nothing to bring us together. Slowly it dawned on me that every monosyllable Mum reluctantly let fall was like a nail in the coffin of my love for her. Where her total silence had taunted and encouraged my longing, the mealy-mouthed conversations we now endured were killing it. Within months of first speaking to her I had given up hoping she would ask after Lisa. I'd admitted to myself that she didn't care where I lived. I was beginning to accept the fact that you can't make someone love you. That's when I started telling myself that I had to change my expectations of Mum.

I don't think I would have managed to do that had Lucy not turned up on my doorstep. In the previous year she had rung from time to time and she never sounded happy. Her marriage wasn't working out. She had no more reason for complaint than Prakash, Ginda or Yasmin, but she'd led a different life from them before she married. She'd had all that freedom, all that going out, and she wasn't as subservient as they were. She didn't even want to accept being stuck in a foreign land all alone except for a husband whom she barely knew and didn't like. It struck me as ironic. She'd conformed, she'd upheld the family honour, but now she felt as lonely and miserable as I'd been.

She'd told Mum and Dad but, of course, they weren't having any of her miseries.

'Stupid girl. Of course you can't come home. Do you not think we have been shamed enough already.' That's what Mum said.

Even though I'd spoken to her about a fortnight before, I was surprised by the state Lucy was in when she arrived with us in Bradford. She didn't give us any warning. It was early evening and Jassey and I were playing in the garden with Lisa when we heard the doorbell ring, long and loud. I went to answer it and there was Lucy on the doorstep, with a suitcase, sobbing. It was some time before she calmed down enough to talk to us, and even then she was edgy and nervous. The phone rang once and you'd think it was a gunshot the way she jumped. She'd run away without her husband knowing. All the way from Germany. It must have taken her months to save the fare.

She sat, nursing her cup of tea in trembling hands and looking completely woebegone. The sassy confidence I'd noticed in Markeaton Park had drained right out of her.

'What am I going to do, Jas?' she asked, and her voice was small and frightened. 'Where am I going to live? I can't go back.'

I had no idea what to say to her. I couldn't remember any women – except widows – living on their own when I was growing up in Mum and Dad's community. I couldn't imagine how I'd have lived through the last six years if I hadn't had Jassey. What place was there for a woman who had left her husband? I thought for ages but in the end, all I could suggest to Lucy was that Mum might have her back.

I couldn't have been more mistaken. I rang Mum later that evening while Jassey was putting Lisa to bed, and she wasn't interested.

'Send her back to Germany at once,' she said. 'She has no business here.'

'But Mum, don't you see, she's unhappy,' I pleaded. 'If you could see how upset she is you'd think differently.'

'Don't tell me what I think. Her place is with her husband. She knows that. Send her back.'

'I can't do that, Mum. She won't have it. She says she'd rather go on the streets than go back.'

'As you wish.' I could hear Mum losing patience with the conversation. 'But if you want to have any place at all in this family I am telling you to send her back. If you don't do that, I'll have nothing more to do with you. You will both be dead in my eyes.'

She hung up and I was left, the receiver dangling useless in my hand, trying to make sense of what she'd said to me. I was back in the wrong. How had that happened? Lucy had left her husband and somehow, in Mum's skewed logic, it was my fault. She'd said I had to choose between her and Lucy. Was her punishment of me never going to stop?

I looked at Lucy. She was exhausted, both physically and emotionally. She was slumped at the table resting her head on her folded arms, like we had to do at St Chad's Infants when we were naughty. Now she sat up and, with her elbows still on the table, she put her chin in her cupped hands and looked at me questioningly. I didn't need to say anything, she could tell by my face.

'She won't have me, will she, Jas? She doesn't want me.'

Her voice was flat and expressionless and, as I shook my head in answer, hers sank back down onto her forearms and she started quietly sobbing. I moved round the table and, gripping her by the shoulders, swung her round to face me.

'You can stop here, if you like, Lucy. You can stay with me and Jassey, help us in the markets. It'd be nice for us to have some family, nice for Lisa to have her *masi* about.'

I meant what I said. I had to because Lucy had no alternative. She had nowhere else to go and no money to get herself back to Germany even if she could have been persuaded to return to her husband. She had no choice and, as I saw it, neither did I. How could I – having suffered six years of rejection from those who were supposed to love and protect me – turn her out?

Even as she was thanking me, a needling inner voice insisted I was ruining any chance I might have had of seeing Dad again. It told me I was making sure Lisa never got to know her grandparents. The voice was right, I knew that. But I shut my ears to it and went upstairs to sort out Lucy's bed.

Lucy's coming to live with us stirred up my life. I was banished by Mum again, as she'd threatened, and Robina went very quiet as well, which really hurt. But at least I had an ally who knew what I was going through. That was consolation, and so was having someone from my family with me all the time. I could see my own sister and it didn't have to be a secret!

When I said she could stop with us I had imagined myself looking after Lucy, caring for my little sister, but as she recovered from the shock of what she'd done and Mum's reaction to it, living with her began to be more like living with a flatmate or a friend. She was fresh and vibrant, she wore different clothes, she was used to going out, she was determined to have fun.

'Who are you meeting?' I asked one Friday evening. I was bathing Lisa, and Lucy was using the bathroom mirror to put her make-up on, getting ready to go out to the pub.

'People from the market, you know . . .' And she reeled off a list of names of people whom I'd smiled at but never said more to than 'How's it going? All right?'

'You should come, Jas. You'd enjoy it. Ask Jassey if he'll babysit, just this once. Come on, it would do you good to go out.'

She was persuasive and I was tempted. Going out had played no part in my life with Jassey, we were always so busy saving for something, striving to prove to ourselves and our families that we could make it without their help. I lifted Lisa out of the bath and onto my lap and together we sat there, watching Lucy paint her lips dark red. I couldn't remember how long it was since I'd worn make-up, since I'd made an effort to make myself look good.

One night, a couple of weeks after that, I did go with her. Jassey was fine about it. He said he was happy to be with Lisa and he didn't want to come; he was pleased to see me having fun with Lucy. I remember rummaging through my clothes trying to find something to wear and thinking everything I owned seemed drab and workaday; in the end Lucy lent me a scarlet blouse with a ruffled front and great big shoulders. She made me put on make-up and showed me how to blow-dry my hair.

'You look beautiful, sweetheart. Enjoy yourself,' Jassey said when I went to say goodbye to him. He was sitting watching telly with Lisa on his lap.

We went to a pub first. There were about ten people in the crowd Lucy had arranged to meet and I knew several of them by sight because they worked in the market. They were all very friendly, asked after Jassey and Lisa, said it was good to see me out from behind my stall. We piled onto a bench that ran around a table; it was hot and close and they were all talking and laughing really loudly. They were arguing about who was the better snooker player, Steve Davis or Jimmy White. I didn't know but it didn't matter. I sat there drinking my Bacardi and Coke and feeling flushed and happy. Late in the evening a girl got up to put the Pet Shop Boys' 'Always on My Mind' on the juke box and we all started swaying and singing along.

When the barman called last orders someone suggested we go on to a nightclub and I was ready for it. We spilled out of the pub and I remember the caress of the warm night air on my face. We linked arms and walked along the pavement and it struck me how strange it felt to be touching anyone who wasn't Jassey or Lisa. I wasn't telling any of Lucy's crowd but I'd never been to a nightclub before. I was twenty-two and for the first time ever I was going dancing. I could have danced down the street.

The nightclub was in a basement and as we walked down the stairs to it I could feel the pounding music through my feet. Loud! I'd never have believed it. Inside it was hot and crowded and exciting. Lights were bouncing off a huge silvery ball suspended above the dance floor which was crammed with people. Lucy grabbed my arm and we pushed our way in, dodging flailing arms, until we found a place for ourselves among all the sweaty bodies. And then we were part of it. The heat, the energy, the sheer physicality of arms, feet, legs, thrusting hips and heads thrown back. Nothing mattered to me then except the music and the movement of my body and the rhythm pulsing through it. 'Born in the USA', 'What's Love Got to Do with It', 'Let's Go Crazy'. We twisted and spun and stamped through the night.

I'd say now that my teenage years began in that nightclub. It was in there I had my first cigarette: Lucy smoked so I did, I thought everything she did was cool. From then on I went out with her most Friday nights and often on Saturdays too, falling into bed with just a couple of hours to go before I'd have to wake up and, bleary-eyed, help Jassey do the weekend markets.

There was always a gang of us; we went drinking, dancing, sometimes to the cinema. It was easy, innocent fun. Jassey always said he didn't mind me going. He never wanted to come and I felt bad about that, but he was insistent. 'You go. Go on, you've worked hard, you deserve it. We're happy here at home, aren't we, poppet?' And he kissed Lisa on the head.

In the next few weeks it was as if I danced the life back into me. On those nights out with Lucy I felt younger, brighter, more light-hearted than I had in years. The new optimism I'd found inside me began to affect me in everyday life. I'd spent so long hunched over my disgrace but now I began to open out and for the first time since fleeing Derby I found I could look the world around me in the face.

That's how I saw Surjit.

He was a market-trader too. He was six foot tall, with black hair and stylish clothes. He was the first man apart from Jassey who'd ever really looked at me, and his gaze was uncomfortably direct.

The first time we went for coffee (it was his suggestion, our stalls were very quiet that day), I told myself that he was only being friendly. The second time I let him hold my hand. The third time he persuaded me to stay on later and have a drink with him, and as we said goodnight he put his hand beneath my jumper and touched my breasts. I felt I'd been shot through with electricity. I half expected his fingerprints to be branded on to me, the mark of my shame.

How could I do that to Jassey? He made it easy for me by trusting me completely. As I told him the lies about where I was going I could hardly bear to look into his kind, innocent face. So much tied me to him: fondness, familiarity, gratitude, duty, mutual responsibility. What drew me to Surjit? I think it was the absence of responsibility. I felt I was having the carefree youth that I'd missed out on. It was like a drug.

Surjit made it easy for me too, at first. I made the rules about when we met and where and what time I had to be back. He respected the fact that I was married and he was very discreet. But after a couple of months that began to change. One night I went to get up and get dressed but he grabbed my wrist and pulled me back down again.

'Stay here tonight,' he said, and there was a harsh edge in his voice that I didn't understand. His grasp twisted and tightened.

'Let go, you're hurting me. You know I can't stay.' I was trying to read his expression but he'd turned his face away from me.

'Suit yourself,' he said, and dropped my wrist, and then he added, really quietly, 'slut'.

I went on seeing him but it was different, he became increasingly possessive. The first time he frightened me we were in a pub. He'd gone to get drinks and while he was at the bar I was looking idly round. The place was packed, but I wasn't conscious of looking at anyone in particular. Surjit said I was though. He came back with the drinks and sat down beside me.

'Like the look of him, do you? You've been staring at him hard enough.'

'Who? What are you talking about? I haven't been looking at anyone.' I was taken aback.

He grabbed my face. He was cupping my chin and his fingers and thumb were pressing into my cheeks as he thrust his face into mine. I tried to pull away but he just pinched harder. 'You're my girl. Got that, *mine*. It's me you look at.'

I was scared of making a scene and even more scared of Surjit's expression, so I just nodded. There wasn't much to say after that. We finished our drinks as quickly as we could but then, as we were walking back down the street, he put his arm around me.

In the weeks that followed memories of the headiest days of our romance clouded my judgement. Surjit became more insistent, more of a bully. He was unpredictable. There was the odd shove, sly pinches that made me cry out with pain. I grew wary in his presence, tense and alert; if he moved suddenly I flinched. I wanted to end it but I didn't know how.

The first time he hit me – 'Tell me, I've got a right to know, do you still sleep with him? *Tell me!*' – his palm was open and the mark of all four fingers was left on my cheek. It was still burning half an hour later when, forcing myself to keep my gaze steady, I told him we had Jassey's family staying, that I'd be too busy to see him the following week.

I couldn't believe how well he took it. 'Okay, babe,' was all he said before, very casually, he went and got a jacket from his bedroom. His insouciance unnerved me.

'What are you doing?'

'I'm walking you home, babe. If I'm not going to see you for a while there's things we need to get sorted. It's about time Jassey and I met. It's only fair a bloke knows who's been screwing his wife.'

'But you can't do that, please don't, you can't.' I was tugging at the sleeve of his denim jacket. An image of bewildered incomprehension on Jassey's loving face flashed into my mind.

'If you're going to leave me, I can do anything I bloody well like, babe. Got that?' he sneered.

That's how Surjit made me stay with him: he reduced our giddy effervescent happiness to a rank display of power. I'd lie beside him, rigid with resentment and self-loathing. I don't know who I despised more, him or myself. Jassey's tenderness taunted me each time I said goodbye to him. He still had no idea of my perfidy and I'd look into his gentle, brown eyes and pray to find a way to keep from hurting him. But of course it was too late.

In the end I told him. Surjit was becoming more violent and irrational. He smashed my windscreen, he followed me like a stalker; one day I found him hiding in the boot of my car. The open-handed slap had long since become the clenched fist and when, during one particularly vicious rage, he broke my nose, I knew I had to end it. I was terrified of him and I couldn't carry the deception any longer. I wanted to confess; I wanted to pay the price for my mad, selfish folly and feel the scourge of Jassey's rage.

I told him one evening when Lisa was in bed, Lucy was out

and we were clearing up our meal. I said the words that made a mockery of all he'd done for me and my heart twisted as I watched the pain of betrayal flood his face. I didn't try to lessen my guilt. I said I'd been having an affair, it had got out of hand and now, much as I wanted to, I couldn't end it. Some instinct stopped me mentioning that Surjit hit me; I'd earlier explained away my broken nose by saying that I'd stood up clumsily and smashed my nose on the stall. I think Jassey would have gone quite mad if he knew someone had hurt me.

When I finished talking he was silent for a long time, staring straight ahead. I tried and failed to read the expression on his face. When eventually he spoke his voice was flat:

'Don't worry. I'll help you. I'll talk to him, we'll sort it out.'

'But aren't you angry? You're supposed to be angry. I thought you'd shout.' The quiet emptiness in his voice was much more devastating than anger would have been. The tears were streaming down his face.

'I'm sorry, Jassey, I'm so sorry, I didn't want to hurt you. Tell me if you're angry, you've every right.'

'I'm not angry.' He stood up so abruptly that his chair clattered to the floor behind him. He kicked it viciously aside and began pacing the room. 'I'm not angry.' He stopped with his back to me, facing the wall, and was still for a few seconds before lashing out with his right foot. It left a dent in the wall, just above the skirting board. 'At least not with you,' he said and, without looking at me, he left the room.

We barely talked about it after that. If I'd wanted a cleansing confessional session it wasn't to be. Jassey never blamed me, never asked for details except what Surjit's name was and where he could be found. A couple of days after I'd told him he left Lucy and me in charge of the Bradford stall and went to where

Surjit worked. Later he told me they'd had it out; it was just a
verbal exchange, nothing violent. 'I've spoken to him, that's the
important thing,' said Jassey. 'Now it will be all right.'

But it wasn't really. Surjit hung around for a while, trying to
cause trouble. He'd turn up at the house, asking to see me. One
Saturday morning he arrived and leant on the bell. I'd seen him
walking up the path and I was cowering upstairs; it was Lucy
who answered. She told me afterwards that he was looking wild-
eyed and mad. When she opened the door, apparently, he took
off his T-shirt. 'He'd shaved his chest hair off, and his whole
chest was covered in blood and scratches. He'd tried to scratch
"Jas" on it with a razor-blade. Can you believe it? I'm sorry, but
you've got to laugh, Jas, talk about daft.' She was enjoying the
re-telling of it.

'Then he opens his hand and he's got this fistful of pills.' Here
Lucy rolled her eyes and moved into melodrama. 'He goes, "Get
Jas down here to see me, or I'll take these." I said, "Hang on
there a minute. I'll get you a glass of water."'

Lucy was chuckling away and I gave a wan smile, trying to
share her amusement. She and Jassey were trying to protect me
from Surjit and I was grateful to them for that. I was doing all I
could to be the dutiful wife. I stopped going to the market in
Leeds, there was too much gossip. Lucy looked after it while I
stayed up in Bradford with Jassey. On the surface we behaved as
if everything was fine but I knew that another small part of our
relationship had died. Jassey was as caring and solicitous as ever
but – and I'm not sure he even realized this – after I told him
about Surjit there was something more muted and automatic
about his affection. He became quieter and less zany. There were
fewer jokes.

And me? I had to accept that I'd made a choice and it had been a very bad one; I'd tried to lead my own life and failed, just like Mum said I would. I felt I was staring into a void. Cursing myself for my ingratitude I looked around me, at the house in Bradford, our successful business, my loyal husband, my healthy, beautiful, enchanting daughter. I vowed to get on with my life.

14

I found I could lose myself in exercise. I'd felt so vulnerable at the first aerobics class I went to, about six months after Lisa was born. My thighs were heavy and my belly was all loose and flabby and I felt hideous. Jassey had suggested I go: I agreed on the condition that he lend me one of his biggest T-shirts so I could cover myself up. He drove me to the class in a local community centre and practically pushed me through the door; I think he was so relieved at the prospect of a solution to one of my problems. He'd kissed me goodbye and said he and Lisa would be back to pick me up when the class was over.

I stuck to the back of the room in that first lesson and while I was waiting for the class to begin my eyes were glued to the floor. I was so scared I'd make a fool of myself. I'd loved netball at school but I'd never done anything remotely sporty since and I was sure everyone else would be lithe and beautiful and know all the steps. When the teacher arrived I was surprised by how friendly and enthusiastic she was. She had a tape recorder with her and she put a Madonna tape into it and started guiding us through a warm-up. I was so busy trying to follow the steps and keep in time that I forgot about feeling self-conscious and by the time 'Like a Virgin' came on and we were skipping on the spot, boxing the air in front of us, I was sweating and breathless but I was really enjoying myself. When the hour came to an end and we were doing our cool-down stretches I sneaked a look round the rest of the class and saw that not all of them were in great shape and there were several faces just as hot and red as mine.

'I'm coming again next week,' was the first thing I said to Jassey when he picked me up.

I tried to go regularly after that; I aimed for once a week but sometimes with the markets and Lisa to see to it was more like once a month. The exercise worked. Slowly but surely I lost all the post-baby fat and, what's more, I found that after each session my mood was lighter; I felt more in control of my life. I recognized the good it was doing me and at the time I was glad of it, but somehow, once Lucy was staying and I started going out, I forgot about aerobics and hardly ever went.

When the affair with Surjit ended I hoped that, once again, exercise might ease my mind and I took up the classes again. I went as often as I could. I even thought about training as a teacher myself and, when I asked the woman who took my classes how to go about it, she said I could begin by helping her out. If a lot of people turned up I'd go up to the front and do the demonstrations with her. She taught me a routine and, as I grew more confident, I asked some of the other regulars in her class if they would let me 'practise' on them. I'd book the hall and whoever turned up would get a free lesson while I got experience. I found that teaching really gave me a buzz.

*   *   *

It was at that time Robina got back in touch. She never explained her silence or said anything about Mum and Lucy, she just rang up one day and started chatting as if we could pick up exactly where she'd left off. And I didn't say anything to prevent that. I was still grasping at the smallest bit of contact my family offered. She was living in Leicester by then; she and Baldev had moved out of his mum and dad's and got their own place; they were doing factory work. Sunny was nearly six; growing up fast, Robina said, 'and full of mischief, morning, noon and night'.

Everything she told me suggested that she was fine, but something about the way she said it niggled at me. She was a bit too reticent for a woman who was leading exactly the life she wanted. (When she questioned me I knew how much misery lay behind my cheerful response, 'Fine, I'm fine', but I certainly wasn't going to add to my shame by telling Robina about Surjit.) There was one call when, right at the end, she went, 'Jas?' and then there was a long pause before she gasped, 'It's just . . . Oh, nothing. I've got to go because Sunny's calling.' She put the phone down so quickly I didn't have time to say goodbye, and afterwards I couldn't stop wondering what she had wanted to tell me.

The next time we spoke she sounded so flat I had to mention it.

'What do you mean? I'm fine,' she said, and changed the subject. We swapped news, mostly about Sunny and Lisa and the funny things they were doing but, try as she might, she couldn't make her voice sound normal. Her unhappiness vibrated through the telephone wire connecting us.

'I tell you what,' I said. 'Why don't I take a day off next week and come down to see you. I'd like to see your place and Sunny will have changed so much since I last saw him.' I had my brightest voice on, like it was going to be a big treat for both of us and, in truth, for me it was: I'd really missed Robina.

The house in Leicester was a flashy place; there was even a built-in bar in the through lounge. But I knew from the moment I walked in that something wasn't right. There was a smashed window in the lounge and the bathroom door had obviously been forced open.

Robina caught my eye, then hurriedly looked away. I'd left Lisa with Eileen so we could talk but Robina wasn't having any of it. She hustled me out of the door with: 'Come on, let's go shopping.'

When I next went it was worse; there were a couple of holes in the wall which must have been made by kicking and there had been no attempt to cover them. I wasn't going to let it go a second time and I asked Robina, straight out, what was happening.

'He just gets angry sometimes,' she said. 'He kicks things.'

'He doesn't hit you, does he?'

'Oh, no, no, *no*,' she said.

The first time I knew for sure something was wrong was when I next went down to Leicester and she met me at the bus station. Sunny was standing beside her, holding her hand, his little hat covering his ears because it was cold. When I went to hug her, she flinched. 'Don't do that . . .'

'What –?'

She glanced down at Sunny and shook her head.

Baldev was at the house when we got there, so we still couldn't talk about it; I had to make conversation with him instead. I'd met him a couple of times before and he had been polite and charming but this time I couldn't wait for him to leave. When at last he did I said, 'What's going on?'

She hesitated. 'Nothing . . .' She flushed and added quickly, 'We just argue a lot.'

'What are you going to do?'

'There's nothing I can do.'

'Do Mum and Dad know?'

'Oh yes,' she sighed. 'I've told them . . .'

And they'd done nothing.

This didn't surprise me. They'd never done anything to help Ginda or Prakash. As far as my mum and dad were concerned, personal happiness wasn't important. What mattered to them was having a daughter who was dutiful and respectable and did nothing to disgrace the family name. 'Heavens, girl, that's what men are like. Why all the fuss?', that's what Mum would say.

'I can't leave him, if that's what you're thinking,' Robina said. She was making us coffee and I noticed she moved her arms really stiffly, as if she was in pain. I knew her reasoning: she was telling herself that she'd chosen Baldev and she had to prove to the community that she could make their union work as well as an arranged marriage.

'I couldn't do it to Mum and Dad, it would destroy them. They're only just now recovering from what happened when you ran away. Mum's just beginning to hold her head up in the *gurdwara*; people who've cut her for years are starting to talk to her. If I left Baldev now, the shame would kill them. And, anyway, what would happen to me? Who would want me after this? I'd be twice divorced. How would I ever get married again?'

'But you can't just put up with it,' I said. 'You *can* leave him. Come and live with me.'

'That's easy for you to say. You don't have to think of the others. When you ran away with Jassey, you didn't think about us.' Her voice was starting to rise. 'You didn't care about your duty, or your family. I'm not the same as you; I still have to put the family first.'

Her words really hurt me, but I tried not to show it. I tried everything to get her to change her mind, but nothing I said seemed to make any difference. Finally I tried to persuade her to have a break, to bring Sunny and come and stay with us for a few days.

All she said was, 'I can't do that. Baldev would be upset and I don't want to hurt him.'

She wanted the marriage to work and she wanted the support of the family, people whose opinion she valued. I had to face the fact that, despite our companionship, what I thought didn't matter because I'd been disowned. The last thing I said to her as I was climbing back on the bus was, 'Go back and tell Mum how bad it is. Show her the bruises. If you won't tell her the truth for your own sake, do it for Sunny.'

A few days later she rang me, sounding much stronger. She'd spoken to Mum and this time, as far as Robina was concerned, Mum had been helpful. She was getting the community leader to come and talk to Robina, to help her sort things out. 'He'll know exactly what to do; he's so wise. That's what Mum said.'

I knew exactly who she meant and my heart sank. I remembered him coming round to Dale Road when I was little and Dad practically bowing as he poured him out a whisky. Like everyone in the community, Mum and Dad would call on him if they needed paperwork doing for a visa to India or something like that. He endorsed everything, and what he said went.

He really mattered to Mum and Dad but as far as I was

concerned he was into all the things – caste, forced marriage, the importance of honour – which I think are wrong. I wanted to say that to Robina, but she wasn't in the mood to listen; if Mum had said Father Christmas was the man to talk to she'd have headed straight off to Lapland. She was staying at Mum and Dad's until the meeting and I said I'd meet her there just beforehand. I wanted to encourage her to tell the community leader everything; I was concerned that she'd be trying to save face by making light of it.

I didn't really think about it until I got to Dale Road, but Robina was taking a big risk allowing me to go there and we were both very nervous. When I arrived she checked the coast was clear before letting me in at the back. Then she locked the door and drew the curtains. It was seven years since I'd been in my parents' house and it felt very strange. It didn't feel like I was coming home; not at all. Everything was familiar: Dad's cup and saucer on the draining board, the worn linoleum, the picture of Siri Guru Granth Sahib on the wall, but I felt disconnected from it. I didn't have time for reminiscences anyway because my focus was on Robina. She looked worn out and sad and a bruise was ripening on her face beneath her make-up.

We'd hardly had time to talk at all when the doorbell rang. She panicked, I panicked; there would be trouble for both of us if I was found there. She got me by my arms, shoved me into the pantry under the stairs and slammed the door shut. It was quite cold and full of the smell of food and spices, sharp pungent smells that brought the memories flooding back to me. We used to hide in there when we played hide-and-seek. Now I crouched down, trying to stay hidden. There was all sorts of junk on the floor, shoes and suitcases and stuff, and it was hard to find a steady footing.

I heard Robina let the community leader in. I could picture him strutting like a peacock, filled with self-importance, his big stomach swelling beneath his suit and tie. He got straight to the point; he wouldn't waste pleasantries on a hapless young woman.

'Well, here I am. Tell me what's wrong.' I could easily hear him through the wall. He was speaking loudly and clearly in very good English.

Robina started talking very fast and she soon burst into tears. To my surprise she was being quite open. 'I'm scared of him.'

'Why?'

'He gets so angry.'

I heard his voice again, talking now in Punjabi. 'These things happen. When men get angry, you have to be calmer. When a pan of milk is boiling up, it's a woman's job to settle it down again.'

'But I'm scared of him. What if he hurts me? Should I not leave him, for the sake of my little boy?'

'No! For the sake of your little boy and for the sake of your family you must stay with your husband. And for your own sake too. Where would you sit without your husband? Stop snivelling and go back to him. You know what happened when your sister ran away from home. You saw how that nearly destroyed your parents.'

I almost lost my balance when I heard that. I wanted to jump out of the pantry and slap that smug, self-righteous creature. I hated him for dragging me into it, for using me as a weapon against Robina.

'If you leave your husband, it will kill your parents – just when they are starting to get back their respect. Think about your family name. Do you want to bring more shame on your family?'

Robina went very quiet. All she'd wanted was for the rows to stop and to have some reassurance that she would be supported by her family. What she was getting was reinforcement of all her worst fears from a man of stature, a man who was speaking for the people she loved, and the whole community where Mum and Dad had to live. How could she not listen?

I was having to strain harder to hear now, because the community leader had dropped his voice and was talking more quickly. I heard him advise her again to go back to Leicester. I couldn't hear anything from Robina. Then they began to move towards the front door. It was easy to distinguish the sounds of their footsteps: her slow, sad shuffle, his confident and heavy tread.

I crept out of the pantry, expecting to talk the whole thing through, but Robina was running around like a demented person, getting her things together.

'What are you doing?' I said.

'I'm going back.'

'You can't go back.'

'You heard him. I have to.' She was crying her eyes out. I stood at the foot of the stairs watching her tears splash onto the little bag she was packing. I wanted to hold her, to draw her to me and keep her safe, but I knew she wouldn't have it.

'You will call me, won't you, if you need anything?'

'Yeah, I will.' She tried to smile through her tears. 'I better go now, I'll have to hurry if I'm going to get home before Baldev.'

She did call me, just a couple of days later. I was surprised to hear from her so soon, and even more surprised by what she had to say me. She asked me if I'd ring Navtej, Sunny's father.

'Of course I will, but why? What do you want me to say to him?'

'I've tried to ring him myself. You know he's still in Canada? I've got through a couple of times but when he answers and I hear his voice I just freeze up. I can't bring myself to speak to him. Will you do it for me, Jas?'

'I've said I will. But you still haven't told me what you want from him.'

'Nothing. I don't want anything from him, not in the way you think. But I'd like Sunny to know his dad; boys need their dads and it's so long since they've seen each other.'

15

I liked doing the weekend markets. They were busy, but the customers were more relaxed and there was always the hint of a party in the atmosphere. Jassey and I had friends among the other stallholders and before the rush started we'd stand round chatting and warming our hands round mugs of coffee. Some of them had children the same age as our Lisa and on Saturdays and Sundays she'd come along with us and she and the other kids would run around amongst the stalls.

On the Sunday after I'd spoken to Robina about Navtej we were at Cannon Mills just outside Bradford, when Lizzie ran up to our stall. Her hair was everywhere, her face was flushed and she was so breathless that it was a minute or two before she could speak. 'Your mum's rang,' she gasped. 'It's your sister, Robina . . .'

She didn't have to finish the sentence. Everything about her spoke of something terrible. I headed straight for the phone box. My hand was shaking as I dialled. Mum picked up almost at once.

'*What's happened?*'

She said, 'It's Robina . . . She died . . . She's dead.'

My brain refused to process this. *No* . . . Robina was my living, breathing, vibrant elder sister; she was part of me . . . We'd shared a bed, we'd walked to school together, she bought me clothes for my wedding, I'd seen her just a week ago. 'What do you mean, dead? How has she died, Mum?' The words came out mechanically. I was on autopilot.

There was a pause. I thought I heard a sob. 'She's committed suicide. She set herself on fire and died in hospital.'

The world seemed to stop.

My legs went weak and I felt completely hollow. Numb with shock, I stood there listening to this really weird, sub-human noise. Then I realized it was howling, and it was coming out of me. I steadied myself against the wall and said, 'Mum, I'm coming to Derby. Right now.'

'No.' She said it really loudly. 'Don't come to Derby. Don't come here; don't show your face here. You'll just make things worse.'

'Mum. Robina is dead. Are you not going to let me come to the house?'

'No. You will make it worse.' She hesitated. 'You can come when it's dark and nobody is here.'

I said, 'Mum, please . . .'

'No. I'm telling you, you'll make it worse.'

I went anyway. We packed up the stall, Lisa went back to Leeds with Lizzie and Jassey drove me down to Derby. Lucy came with us but no one said a word for the entire journey. Jason Donovan's 'Too Many Broken Hearts' was playing on the radio, over and over again. I hate that song now.

Could I have saved Robina? That's all I was thinking. Should I have guessed she was thinking of suicide? No one can answer that question, but the guilt still twists inside me.

When we got to my mum and dad's house the mourners were all there; I could hear the women wailing as I opened the front door. They were all in the living-room where there was a white cloth spread out on the floor and they were sitting on it, crying and beating themselves with their hands. There were about fifteen of them, including my sisters and some others that I thought I recognized but I'd been away so long I wasn't sure.

It was such a shock to suddenly be back amongst them that my head began to swim; for a few moments I thought I might faint. I leant against the door frame. I could feel the heat of Lucy's body pressed close beside me. The room was hot and stuffy and, since we'd stepped into it, completely quiet. All those eyes stared at us, no one said anything, and then, without even acknowledging us, our sisters – Prakash, Ginda and Yasmin – stood up, wrapped their white scarves around their heads, and walked out.

I was stunned.

Robina, our sister, our own flesh and blood, had died a horrible violent death, and they were still punishing me for something that had happened seven years ago.

With a shred of hope still in my heart, I looked at Mum. I wanted to go over and throw my arms around her, because Robina was dead and I needed her and I wanted her to need me. But she just sat there, cold as a stone.

I turned to face Lucy. Her face was a mask of shock and incomprehension. 'There's nothing for us here,' I said. She nodded and we left.

*   *   *

The funeral was in Leicester. I knew they didn't want me there but I went anyway. I was past caring by then. For the mourning beforehand we went to Baldev and Robina's house and the burnt smell made me gag as soon as the door opened. Seeing them all there made me so angry. The community leader, Mum, Dad: she'd asked them for help and they as good as turned their backs on her. They may as well have spat in her face. Now it was too late and they were parading their sorrow: a respectable emotion dressed up in a solemn expression and white mourning dress.

Upstairs in the bedroom there was a great charred mark on the carpet. I couldn't bear to look at it. Baldev stepped back as I approached him. 'Why didn't you stop her?' I asked.

Mum had told me it happened when he and Robina were arguing. She told me Robina said she was going to kill herself, then drenched herself with paraffin. Then she'd said again that she was going to set herself on fire.

'Why didn't you stop her?' I asked again.

'What could I have done? She lit the match and her suit caught on fire.'

By the time the ambulance arrived, she had suffered ninety per cent burns, but she was still conscious, that's what they told me. 'Please cover my face,' she'd whispered as she was carried across the pavement and into the ambulance. With her dying breath she tried to spare Mum and Dad's shame.

Her casket was laid out in the living-room. She was so disfigured that, against all tradition, it was closed. There was a photograph on top instead. Regardless of what anybody else thought I picked it up so I could have one long last look at my darling sister. Mum always taught us not to smile in photographs, but Robina was looking right into the camera and you could see the light of laughter in her eyes. She might have expected her family to cherish and protect that light, but they didn't. Mum, Dad, the community leader . . . between them they stamped it out.

16

It didn't sit with me that Robina would take her own life and I was determined not to leave it there. The only person who knew the truth was Baldev and he would only say over and over again: 'I've told you, she said she was going to set herself on fire, but I didn't believe her. She lit the match and her suit caught the flame.' Robina may have made a cry for help but a kind word from someone, a consoling arm, would have stopped her. I was sure she never meant to die. My anger and grief made me want to see Baldev punished.

I thought about it for a bit and then I told Mum what I felt. I'd turned a corner in my head by then. Her rejection of me at the time of Robina's death changed things. I considered the game she'd been playing for so long, taunting me by withholding her affection and acceptance, and I thought, 'Why am I still playing a part in this? What more can I lose?' I realized then that in order for me to live, something inside me had to die. I still yearned to be part of my family, but I wasn't going to let it rule my life.

When I rang Mum my only thought was for Robina. 'I want

to find out what really happened that day. Will you come with me to a solicitor?'

She said she would. She barely hesitated before agreeing and I wondered afterwards if she was glad of a chance to right the wrong she'd done Robina. Jassey and I came in the car to get her and that was the first time that she met him. I'd longed for that meeting to happen but when it did – her sitting beside him as he drove though the streets of Derby – it didn't matter to me any more. It had come too late.

From the Yellow Pages I chose a solicitor, picked out because the company name wasn't Asian. Jassey waited in the corridor while we went inside. Mum sat beside me, both of us on hard chairs opposite this great big desk; me translating everything into Punjabi so she could understand it. When I asked her to confirm things – did Robina tell her what Baldev was like? – she said very meekly, 'Yes'.

She was so quiet and compliant that I couldn't believe she was the same hard, stubborn, mouthy woman I had known all my life. And it wasn't just when we were in the solicitor's office. It seemed to me that the day Robina died Mum turned into a mouse. Her only interest was in Sunny. She took him in; she even got herself made legal guardian because she was scared Navtej would come and take him. She and Dad devoted themselves to bringing him up. It can't have been easy for them; their life had slowed down by then and suddenly they were landed with a six-year-old kid. But they did their best and he became the light of my dad's life.

I asked the solicitor if he thought we had a case and he said possibly. In the next few weeks we gave him all the evidence we could. We went to the inquest; Jassey and I took Mum and Dad. One of Robina's neighbours had made a sworn statement saying she heard Baldev shout, 'You bitch, you bitch, what have you done this time?' shortly before he called out of the bedroom window, 'Fire, fire, get an ambulance.' She said she'd heard them rowing in the past.

The forensic scientist who went to the house saw signs of fighting. His statement said the available information suggested that 'a disturbance between Mr and Mrs Basi took place in the through lounge'. He saw a coffee table on its side and a broken wall plate lying on the floor. He also mentioned a hole 'apparently caused by kicking' by the side of the lounge door.

Baldev's statement said he had stayed out all day and come home to find Robina crying. Then they'd had a row. He said he used a bed quilt to smother the flames that were eating at my sister. Could he have been quicker with it, that's what I wanted to know. The pathologist's report said Robina had extensive third degree burns to ninety-five per cent of her body.

The coroner gave an open verdict. That upsets me to this day. No one was held accountable for Robina's death. There was no evidence to suggest it wasn't suicide.

Mum never told the others – Prakash, Ginda, Yasmin and Balbir – what we did. After her death Robina was never spoken of at all. My guess is that Mum kept quiet about going to see the lawyer because she didn't want them to know she was talking to me. I accepted that. I was still playing by her rules so I didn't embarrass her. I knew she was afraid to let other people know she was talking to me, lest they should think she condoned my behaviour. She was afraid of the gossip in the *gurdwara* and among the neighbours, and afraid that my sisters would say, 'If you want to talk to her, don't talk to us.' She didn't want the family's good name tainted by my dishonour, and I accepted that because I had to; I'd rather see my mum and dad in secret than not at all.

It led to some absurd situations. Several times when I was visiting, one of my sisters would arrive and I'd have to rush upstairs and hide in a bedroom. Once Mum rang and asked me to come round because Sunny was sick. In her panic she rang Gin as well but she forgot about that until we heard the front door click shut and Gin call out 'Mum?'

'Go! Quick! Get out of here! Go!' Mum was shooing me out as if I was a chicken.

'But where? Where do you want me to go?'

'Anywhere! Out through the back door. Go out the back.'

I went out the back door and hid behind the outside toilet while I decided what to do next. I was scared Gin would see me through the living-room window if I went through our front gate, so I climbed the wall into our next-door neighbour's garden and went out that way. I jumped through hoops because I was scared that if I got found out I'd lose the little bit of Mum and Dad I had.

I cared about that but I didn't care if my family found out that I was house-hunting in Derby. Jassey and I had decided we weren't going to stay in exile any more. It was supposed to be a fresh start for us, away from all that had happened in Bradford and Leeds. The markets are a close community and Jassey felt humiliated by the other traders knowing about my affair with Surjit. Lucy wasn't living with us any more, she'd rented her own place in Leeds and I think Jassey hoped too that a move might rekindle our romance.

The house I eventually found was another step up for us. It was detached, with four bedrooms and two bathrooms. There was a great big living area divided by a real log fire and with patio doors out onto the garden. It even had a greenhouse where I grew tomatoes. We'd started with nothing and that house was what we achieved. No one helped us. No one gave us a thing. My sisters, Jassey's siblings, they would have had financial – as well as emotional – support from our families, but everything we did, we did alone. And compared to the rest of them we were well-off by the time we came back to Derby. 'Without us, you'll be rolling round in the gutter.' That's what Mum said when I was a sobbing teenager in Newcastle, and we'd proved her wrong.

She never acknowledged that, of course, never said she was impressed by what we had achieved, although she must have been. She came to the house two or three times, and Dad did too. In a strange way I think she felt she owed that to me, like it was payback for the way I'd tried to get justice for Robina. But those visits didn't mean much. We never got past 'how are you' or 'did you see that on television' and there were long, unbearable silences. Lisa was the only bridge between us, the little person in the middle who kept the conversation going. I was glad she was finally getting to know her grandparents but still, I was relieved when they stood up and said it was time to go home.

I found Dad's presence warming, just as I always had done, but he was still Mum's silent shadow and the relationship between her and me was very brittle. There were so many things I wanted to ask her: 'How could you have told me I was dead in your eyes?' 'How could you have turned Robina away?' 'How could you not have been there for me when I had Lisa?' Those questions were such a big part of me, but they were never mentioned, she just didn't want to go there. From my point of view they sat between us like a rock.

She let me go to her house though, me and Jassey. The irony

was that, as time went on, those two got on better than me and
Mum did. She saw he was a good man in the way he supported
me through the business about Baldev, and once she got over the
fact of his caste she liked him.

I bumped into Ginda on a couple of my visits to Mum and
Dad's house. Her marriage was going through such a bad patch
at the time that she was stopping there. The first time it
happened I was in the living-room talking to her kids, Sereena
and David, when she walked in. I immediately got up to leave
because I thought that's what Mum would have wanted but, to
my surprise, Ginda started talking to me.

'Nice house you and Jassey have got yourself now. I bet that
cost a packet,' she said.

'Yeah, well . . .' I smiled and looked away. She hadn't spoken
to me for so many years and I wasn't certain of the ground
between us.

'You heard about me and your brother-in-law? Mum told you
that I left him?'

Her tone had changed and I knew then that this was going
to be about her not me. We talked for a bit and she was so full
of miseries that I couldn't help but feel sorry for her. She'd
done everything right: made the marriage Mum and Dad
wanted and conformed to all the invisible but oppressive rules
laid down by 'the community', but I could see now that it
hadn't given her a special pass to happiness. She was part of
our family in a way I'd never be but, beyond that, her life
didn't look fantastic.

I listened to Ginda and heard her complaints and they took me
back down the years to those terrible Sundays when I was little. I
knew then without doubt that in running away from my arranged marriage I'd done the right thing. At least I got to make

my own choices and decisions. Where on earth would I have been if I had stayed?

I was walking in town a few days later when a woman stepped out of a bus queue and touched my arm.

'I thought you were dead.' That's what she said as she stopped me.

I didn't recognize her at first, she was standing behind a pushchair with a crowd of small children at her feet; I guessed she was about forty. I must have looked blank, because she said, 'I'm Habiba. Habiba Ahmed. Remember?' Then she smiled, a big smile that showed a gap between her front teeth.

A memory flashed through my mind of me standing in the playground at Littleover School and watching a giggling Robina trying to measure that gap with a ruler. She and Habiba had been great friends although Robina was always a bit in awe of her because she was so clever, the sort that got her work read out in assembly. I looked down at the children, five of them, and up again into the tired, worn face of their mother.

'Habiba! Of course! Of course I recognize you. But I'm not dead. Whatever made you think. . . .' Suddenly I realized her mistake. I put my hand on her arm. 'It was Robina who died.'

'No. I know that and I'm so sorry, so very sorry. Her death was a terrible thing.' She paused, embarrassed, but then pressed on. 'I thought you were dead also. I thought you died years ago, that's what they told us.'

It was on the tip of my tongue to say 'who told you?' but I decided against it. 'Dead in her mother's eyes!' 'Dead, I'm telling you.' I could imagine the whispers that slithered through the *gurdwara* after I ran away. I forced a laugh.

'No, here I am, alive and breathing. And how about you, Habiba? How are you? Did you go to college?'

'No, Jasvinder, I didn't.' She gave a sad little smile. 'I was fifteen when I married and then, you know how it is, we needed money to bring my husband over. Then he came and we had Aabid.' She ruffled the head of the tallest child, who was leaning against her. 'Then the others. I'm lucky, my husband is a good father.'

17

I worked to make that house in Derby a home for us. I decorated the rooms in strong, vibrant colours, painting them myself because I liked doing it; the simple repetitive action soothed my mind and left me too tired to think. I found I loved gardening and I filled the garden with flowers, and even planted a few vegetables. We had all that we wanted but since moving back to Derby we were finding it hard to earn the money to support our new life. We'd made such a success of the markets in Leeds and Bradford and we'd just assumed it would be easy to carry that on in Derby, but it didn't happen. We had all the expertise, but by then the hunger . . . the drive . . . the partnership didn't exist between us. It soon became clear that there wasn't enough work for both of us, so I looked into setting myself up as an aerobics teacher. Another bond was broken.

We held it together, for Lisa's sake. She was at school by then and loving it. Come three o'clock I'd be waiting at the gate and she'd come running out, her cardigan dangling off her shoulders, full of all she'd done that day, waving some still damp picture. For all she knew, we were still a happy family. Most people, looking at us, would have thought so, but the fact was Jassey and I didn't even share a bedroom any more. We couldn't even pretend we had that between us.

We never argued but we didn't communicate either, we just co-existed, leading our separate lives in the house we'd worked so hard for. The way we were reminded me of how Mum and Dad had been: soldiering on alone together. Should that have been enough for me? Should I have been satisfied? Jassey was. He said so. 'Don't leave me sweet, please. We're all right like this. We can still share our life together.' That's what he pleaded.

Sometimes I'd look at Mum and think that Robina's death must have done her actual, physical damage because from the day it happened she dwindled. It wasn't just that she became this new cowed, quiet person; I watched her getting smaller. She lost so much weight it looked like she was shrinking. She'd been so dominant in that house and now it seemed somehow empty, as though a life force had been sucked out of it.

She'd always been a great one for ailments: a strange ache here, an unexplained twinge there, and the doctor's was like a Mecca for her. She loved going up there, and coming back home with a new diagnosis and a bottle of pills. But now she really did seem ill. As far back as I can remember, when my mum sat it was always on the floor by the fireplace – I can see her in my mind's eye now, sitting there, cross-legged, dealing with her vegetables. But there came a time when that seemed like too much effort for her. She preferred to sink back on the old worn sofa-bed. She'd sit there holding her mug of tea – she needed two hands to keep it steady by that time – and she seemed to have retreated into a world of her own. Dad hovered around the living-room, wanting to help, uncertain what to do, his brow furrowed with anxiety, his head nodding as he mumbled on in endless conversation with himself.

The GP thought it was gallstones Mum was suffering from and he sent her to the hospital to have them removed. That's when they told her she had bowel cancer. The doctor who confirmed the diagnosis said it was terminal.

I went to see her more and more often. It was a relief to be out of our house, anyway. I never went without ringing first, because I didn't want to embarrass her by arriving when my sisters were there, but it soon became apparent that I didn't need to worry. They weren't regular visitors. Sometimes she'd ring and ask me to come, if she needed a letter written, or she wanted help with a phone call, or with filling in a form. Other times I'd drop in and make her and Dad a cup of tea; I'd check the cupboards and, if necessary, I'd go up to the shop and get some food in for them.

It sounds callous, but it wasn't love of her that made me go there. I had special feelings for my dad, but it was a sense of duty that made me care for Mum; duty and the fact that after all those years I had what I wanted: I was allowed to see my parents, they agreed to have me in their home. I wouldn't have said I was back in the family, but I wasn't a complete outcast any more.

I don't know what Mum was feeling. She never said much. She accepted what I did for her, but I had no idea what was going on in her head. The only hint she ever gave me came one day when I was bathing her. I did that quite often because, although Dad was there to care for her, he was also quite frail and lifting Mum in and out was too much for him even though there was almost nothing of her by then.

I was glad to give her a bath, because the warm water seemed to soothe her. She'd want me to wash her hair but it nearly broke my heart to do that. She'd always been so proud of her long thick hair and so particular about dyeing it, but now it was grey and sparse and, when I washed it, great clumps came out and the limp strands twined round my fingers as I tried to hide them from her.

I used to make excuses not to wash her hair and then she'd lie back with her eyes shut and it was as if the heat of the room eased the tired, tense lines from her face. I'd let her soak there a while and then, when I started to worry she'd get cold, I'd help her out onto the mat. She was so light it was no trouble. Usually she didn't say much, but the day I have in mind she suddenly said, 'This is wrong. It should be the other way round.'

She said it very quietly and with real humility and I knew what she meant by it. It was her way of saying, 'I'm the mother, you're the daughter, I should be looking after you.' That's the only time I ever thought she might regret all that she'd done to me. I didn't answer her. I couldn't; I was too choked up. I pretended I hadn't heard as I stood her on the bathmat to get her dry. Then I dressed her in a pink flannel nightdress and Dad's old brown cardigan and took her downstairs to settle her in the armchair the hospital had provided. And all the time I was thinking, 'You've wasted so much time.'

The first thing I ever told Rajvinder was that I was going to see my mum. He worked in the garage where I used to fill my car with petrol and he was on the till the day I met him. I went up to the counter to pay and I was writing out my cheque, deep in thought, when I suddenly realized he was talking to me. I started.

'Sorry, I wasn't listening. What did you say?'

'Only asking where you're off to, dressed like that.' His voice was friendly and full of confidence.

'I'm off to work. I'm an aerobics teacher and I'm going to take a class.' I smiled as I passed him the cheque and something made me add: 'But first I'm going to see my mum, she's not been well.'

'Sorry about that,' he said, making it sound as if he really was sorry. 'I hope she's better soon.'

That was that really. I got back in the car and drove off but there was something about the memory of our encounter that I couldn't shake off. He had an infectious grin and the most fantastic eyes, that's what stuck with me. He had long, long eyelashes and his eyes were so sparkling and full of life. It was more than two years since my affair with Surjit had ended and in all that time I'd kept my head down, trying to stay strong and get my life in order. Even when I finally accepted that my marriage had no future I hadn't given a second's thought to meeting anybody else. Now I noticed, with a complicated mixture of excitement and distress, that I felt a tingle of anticipation.

I was back at the garage the following week. The same man was there and he remembered me. I tried not to show how pleased I was. He waved from his place behind the counter while I was filling the car and then, as soon as I went inside, he said, 'How's your mum, then? I hope she's a bit better.'

'Not really, but thanks for asking anyway. She keeps losing weight, and I know my dad's worried; he looks so tired and . . .' I stopped mid-sentence, suddenly unsure why I was blurting out all this to a stranger.

'That's a shame. I bet they're glad to have a daughter like you looking out for them,' he said. 'Is it far for you to go?'

We talked on for a bit in between his serving customers, easy, inconsequential conversation. He told me he was running the garage for his dad, who owned it. As I turned to leave he said, 'I'm Rajvinder Sanghera, by the way. Friends call me Raj.'

'Right.' I smiled. 'I'm Jasvinder Kaur, but everyone calls me Jas.'

Filling up with petrol became a highlight of my week. I wasn't thinking of romance, it was Raj's friendship I appreciated. There is no lonelier place to live than in a dying marriage. I was creeping round our house, struggling for breath in the emotional vacuum that surrounded us. Guilt tormented me, seeping through my mind, spreading itself like a foul slick of oil over all my moods and feelings. I was frightened of the future. If I stayed I felt sure I would wither and die, but I was terrified of leaving. Raj's friendliness, his interest in me and his concern all acted like a balm on the persistent ache inside me. I'd turn away from his till after five, ten, fifteen minutes' conversation and, walking back to my car, realize that I still had a smile on my face.

I told him the situation I was in with Jassey and he was very sympathetic. He said he understood my feeling torn apart because he was recently divorced himself. The more I learnt about him, the more I liked him. He was twenty-six, just a year older than me, and he seemed very sure of himself. He was charming and he had a lovely sense of humour which, at that time, I really valued; it felt so good to have someone to laugh with.

Mum's bed had been moved downstairs into the living-room by then. With that and the commode the hospital sent it looked just like a sickroom. Mum had a colostomy bag and she hated it. The first thing she said whenever I went in to see her, was 'Does it smell in here?' and I'd say 'No, Mum, it doesn't, don't worry about that'. But it did; the sour stench of sickness tainted the house and the lavender air freshener that she sprayed everywhere did nothing to disguise it. I'd arrive and find Dad wandering aimlessly from room to room; in the face of Mum's decay he seemed lost.

I should never have told them that my marriage was collapsing. Mum was too frail and sick, she didn't need the worry and nor did Dad. But after all the years of separation, secrecy and evasion I wanted them to know me – and accept me – as I was. I knew they were reluctant, but I made them listen.

'I don't love him, Mum. I've tried and tried to, but I don't.'

She struggled to lift herself off her pillows, angered into forgetting her failing body, eager to bring the dignity of height to her tirade against my folly. But her arms were too weak, they wouldn't hold her and she wouldn't let me help her. She turned her face from me and with all the contempt she could muster spat out, 'Love!'

Why did I expect her to understand me? She was Jagir Kaur, who, at the age of fifteen, had been made to marry her dead sister's husband, my father. She had worked hard, raised eight children and led her life according to the unspoken rules of the community she feared and treasured. What did she care for love?

I hadn't meant to tell her about Raj, but in the end I did because I needed something to refute her belief that I was mad to consider walking out on a good man like Jassey. I wasn't afraid of her any more but I still longed for her to respect the choices I made and the way I lived my life. She made no comment, I wasn't even sure she had taken it in, but a few days later when I was helping her to drink a cup of tea she pushed my hand away and said, 'I had a dream last night about the man you want to marry.'

'What man?' I said.

'The man you've been seeing. The man you are leaving your husband for.'

'I'm not leaving Jassey *for* anyone, Mum, I'm leaving him because . . .'

'I dreamt you married this man and he brought you nothing but unhappiness. I dreamt you got divorced.'

'Well, you can forget your dream. I'm not planning on marrying anyone.'

That was the truth. I tried to keep the anger out of my voice, but it's what I felt. My relationship with Raj had gone beyond friendship but marriage, to him or anyone else, was the last thing on my mind. I thought Mum was just up to her old manipulative ways and I ignored her. I never for one moment thought she might be right.

18

I didn't plan to take much with me when I left Jassey. I packed a single case with nothing more in it than a few clothes for me and Lisa. When the day came, I aimed to leave quickly.

It was about 6 p.m. one weekday. Once Lisa had finished her tea I took her by the hand and we walked out through the front door and I didn't look back. I remember the hot, sticky feel of her fingers crushed in mine and the confusion in her voice as she kept asking, 'Where are we going?' I ignored her question and held her hand too tight as I hurried her along, the suitcase banging against my legs as I tried to escape from the terrible sobbing behind us. I can bring the desperate misery of that sound to mind as if I heard it yesterday, and the memory of the pain I caused still makes me wince. Lisa's little face, pinched and frightened, trying to be brave as she said goodbye to her daddy. 'But can't he come with us, Mummy?' And Jassey, my knight in shining armour, broken. Ten years before he'd rescued me and now, in return, I'd left him weeping.

We went to Raj's house and as far as everyone was concerned that confirmed me as the baddy. When he offered me a place to stay and said Lisa could come too, I knew I had no alternative. And once we got there it was easy to live with that decision because he did his best for us. We arrived, pale and shattered, and he was at his most disarming: gently solicitous but also very funny. He even managed to make Lisa giggle.

That's how he was in the weeks and months that followed and gradually, as he wrapped me round with his affection, I began to let go of my guilt and allow myself to fall in love with him. It's what I wanted. I craved affection and the safety of a relationship. For all my wilfulness I felt too vulnerable to survive alone. I yearned for a solid respectable marriage that would allow me to hold my head up high. I'd always despised the strict censoriousness of Mum and Dad's community, but in the years alone with Jassey I'd come to understand that it did afford a safe place in the world, a clear pattern, and I'd found nothing to replace that. I wanted to show the people I'd come back to live among that I wasn't worthless.

I never introduced Raj to Mum. It seemed bitterly ironic but, just as I'd found someone Mum and Dad could really have approved of – a *jatt*, like us, a dutiful Asian son running his father's business – they decided to acknowledge their *chamar* son-in-law. Mum thought the world of Jassey by then.

'You won't take the house from him, will you?' That's what she kept saying once I'd left him. The first time it came up, I pointed out that I'd worked hard for the house too, it hadn't all been down to Jassey, but Mum ignored that. 'Please, Jasvinder, don't take it from him. Think of me, you know I'm dying, let me go to my grave knowing that my daughter has done the right thing. Please, for my sake, say you'll let that poor man keep the house.' She was so insistent that I soon agreed to what she wanted. Losing the security didn't bother me. I'd learnt how to make money; I was confident that I could work my way up again. What hurt was that, yet again, Mum couldn't find it inside herself to give me her backing.

Lisa took her dad's side too. At first she seemed quite happy stopping with me at Raj's. We did her room up nicely. He paid attention to her, he taught her how to ride a bike; one weekend the three of us went to EuroDisney. I'll never forget the look on Lisa's face when she saw Mickey Mouse.

But she never really settled. She often asked about Jassey. 'Does Dad have anyone to eat his dinner with?' or 'Do you think Dad has anyone to talk to?' She'd say those things looking up at me with her clear, brown-eyed gaze and, as I scrabbled for an answer, I hated myself for putting her in a position where she had to think like that. I wasn't surprised when, one night as I was putting her to bed, she said, 'Mummy, would it be all right if I went to live with Daddy for a bit? I would miss you. But you've got Raj to look after you and Daddy's got no one, he says he's lonely by himself.'

My heart lurched. I'd foreseen this moment and I'd been dreading it. I wanted to grab Lisa and clutch her to me, rest my cheek on her silky, sweet-smelling hair and feel the warm weight of her solid little body on my lap. I didn't though. Willing myself not to cry, fighting the lump that was forcing its way up my throat, I bent forward, smoothed her hair and kissed her on the cheek.

'Course you can, if that's what you really want. I'll talk to your dad about it in the morning.'

I rang Jassey and he was delighted. We agreed that, as a trial, she should stop with him for a week, starting the next Saturday when his usual access visit was due. When the time came to leave her there I wouldn't let myself hug her for any longer than usual;

I didn't want her to know that letting her go was tearing me apart. But after I'd dropped her off the days dragged by; the week seemed to last for ever. I'd made Jassey promise to let me know if she was missing me, but I didn't hear a thing.

The following Friday at 5 p.m. – our normal handover time – I parked outside my old house and ran up the path to the door. I'd been half hoping to find Lisa waiting for me, her face pressed against a downstairs window, but she wasn't there. I rang the bell and waited but no one came. I tried again, leaning on it a little longer this time. Still no response. I made my way round the house, peering into any windows I could reach, and then I called into the back garden in case they were there. Nothing.

I checked my watch. It was quarter past five. Either I'd got the time wrong or Jassey had kept her out late. Annoyed, I got back in the car and settled down to wait. At six o'clock I went back to the house and rang the bell again, and this time I rapped on the door as well. I knew that was madness because they couldn't have gone back in without me seeing them, but I had to do something. That's what made me drive the few streets to the nearest phone box and dial Jassey's number. As I expected, there was no reply. I checked my watch again, trying to ignore the prickle of panic that was creeping over me.

When I told Raj he was all for not fussing, but I couldn't help it. I went back to check the house at eight and nine o'clock and then, really frightened, I rang Jassey's mum.

'But he's in India, he went three days ago.'

'So where's Lisa?'

'She's with him of course. He's taken her to meet her relatives.'

'Lisa! In India?' I could hear a sharp note of hysteria in my voice. 'When's she coming back? Why didn't Jassey tell me?'

My mother-in-law's voice was cool. 'Lisa is his daughter, Jasvinder. He can take her to meet her family if he wishes.'

It was almost three weeks before they came back and in all that time I didn't hear from them. I was beside myself with worry and confusion. I missed Lisa desperately and I found it so hard to believe that Jassey, who for years had done all he could to protect me, would now do something so unfair.

I went round the day they were due back in Derby but Jassey wouldn't let me take her home with me. 'She's not a parcel, Jas. We can't keep moving her about the place. She likes it here with me.'

They were standing in the doorway. Lisa was leaning up against him, wearing a little embroidered top that he must have bought in India. I noticed that her hair had grown and that, behind her big bottle glasses, she looked tired. I opened my mouth to argue or plead, I'm not sure which, but then I closed it again. She loved us both and I didn't want to fight in front of her. I knelt down and gave her a kiss and a hug and then, turning to leave, I said, 'Have it your own way, Jassey. I'm going to talk to a lawyer!'

When our case eventually came to court, Jassey got residence. The court said Lisa was used to living with her father and it would be unfair to unsettle her again. I was to be allowed access one night a week and on alternate weekends. Those words landed on me like hammer blows. I didn't speak to anyone as I left the court. I don't know how I got home; I must have driven but I've no recollection of the journey. I just remember sitting on the bed in the room that Raj and I had made nice for Lisa and holding the pillow up to my face so I could smell her smell. My arms ached to hold her. My mind was a kaleidoscopic mess of all the moments in her life I now wouldn't share. I visualized her woken by a nightmare, trying out make-up, getting her first period, falling in love . . . all the moments when a girl needs support and guidance from her mum, moments when I wasn't going to be there for her. I wept for my precious daughter and the way I'd let her down.

I cut myself off from Jassey after that; the only way I could cope with the situation was by switching off completely and, unless we had something to say about Lisa, we didn't talk at all. I knew he was going for all the sympathy he could get, and the word on the Asian grapevine was that he deserved sympathy because I'd abandoned him and left him to bring up our child alone. That infuriated me because he knew that I'd have given anything to have Lisa safe with me.

I stuck to the court order though. The only time I broke it was one night when Jassey left Lisa home alone. She rang me about nine o'clock. 'Daddy's gone out again,' is all she said. The telly was on in the background but I could still hear the little tremble in her voice. I told her I'd be there in fifteen minutes.

When I got to the house I knocked on the door, but she didn't come and open it. I knocked again and then I started walking round the house, calling out to her. She appeared at the living-room window, peeping cautiously round the edge of a curtain, but when she saw me relief washed the worry from her face. She let me in and we had a cuddle and then I told her I was going to take her home with me.

She was worried about that: worried that Jassey would be cross with her when he came back and found her gone, worried that the magistrate would be cross with me for taking her. 'She said I could only come to you on Tuesdays in the week and it's Thursday today,' she said, pulling away from me so she could look into my face. She looked so serious, so anxious, and it tugged at my heart that such a little girl should have to think like that, but I did my best to reassure her. I took her home and tucked her into bed and she quickly fell asleep.

It was about 11.30 p.m. when Jassey rang and there was panic in his voice. I hadn't left him a note telling him I'd got Lisa. It was a mean thing to do, I knew that, but I thought he deserved a shock for having left Lisa on her own. He came roaring round once he knew I'd got her. He was hammering on the door and screaming that he wanted Lisa, insisting that he was going to take her home immediately. He was making such a racket that I'm surprised he didn't wake the whole neighbourhood. Thank heavens Lisa didn't wake up.

'She's stopping here tonight, no question,' I said. I was standing at the front door with my arms folded as if I was physically guarding her. 'I'll bring her back after that if you agree never to leave her on her own again.'

He denied he'd done that. 'It was only for five minutes . . .', that was the sort of excuse he was making. But I wouldn't listen. Why should I? If he couldn't cope I would have had her more than gladly. He knew he only had to ask.

19

The time came when Mum was so sick that she was in and out of hospital. I used to take her to appointments and as I helped her down the endless corridors and sat with her in airless waiting-rooms it struck me that, although she'd lived most of her life in England, she was still a stranger stranded in a foreign land. She'd have been totally lost on her own. I could see the panic growing in her if I left her alone for a second, to go to the toilet for instance, or to fetch us both a cup of tea.

My heart used to tilt as I watched her clinging to the shreds of her dignity in the face of the nurses' over-familiar cheeriness and the doctors' L-O-U-D, S-L-O-W E-X-P-L-A-N-A-T-I-O-N-S of the procedures she would have to undergo.

'She's not deaf, shouting at her isn't going to help. She doesn't speak English,' I said, struggling to control my anger as a well-meaning young doctor boomed into her face.

'I'm only trying to help her understand,' he said, rounding on me.

'That's not the way to do it. Would you understand if I

shouted at you slowly in Punjabi? Why don't you speak to me and I'll translate it for her.'

We were both exhausted at the end of those appointments. I'd drive her home and half carry her from the curb to her armchair. I'd do all I could to make her comfortable and then – it still hurts to admit this – if one of my older siblings was coming over I'd have to leave. Only Lucy was allowed to know about my visits. She was there sometimes. Mum and Dad let her come over when she wanted. They never let her move back in again, she had to fend for herself, but still, she was accepted more than I was. Her visits weren't kept secret. When Mum and Dad hustled me out of the house I'd drive home in tears, angry with myself for being so stupid as to care.

A few weeks before she died Mum was given a place in the local hospice. She was in constant pain by then and Dad couldn't look after her properly any more. At first she was put in a room with three other patients; it was a bright, airy room and the others were friendly but they had a problem with Mum's prayers. I had to sympathize. She was still in the habit of putting them on full-blast first thing in the morning and mumbling her own devotions along with the tape recorder. *Ik-cum-kar, ik-cum-kar* – I remembered the dawn chorus from my own child-hood all too well.

The nurses were very kind. They suggested she should play them later or more quietly, preferably both, but the very thought of that made Mum look bewildered and miserable. She was an old lady, wedded to a routine she'd clung to for almost fifty years, and it seemed too cruel that she should lose that comfort in the last weeks of her life. I wanted to spare her that, so I asked the staff if they could move her, if there was any chance they might find her a little room to herself, and after a few days they did.

It was a tiny room, just big enough for a single bed, a bedside table and a high backed armchair. I used to have to bring a chair for myself from another room when I went to visit. I went as often as I could, always going early in the morning or late in the evening when I knew my sisters and brother wouldn't be there. Right to the end she couldn't admit to them that she was seeing me.

She was sitting in the armchair when I arrived one morning about a week before she died. The nurses had put her there, but they hadn't got her dressed, so she was still in her nightdress. It was blue with little flowers on it and long sleeves. She was slumped in her chair, just staring into space, and my first thought was how thin and frail she looked. It was hard to remember her as the strong, unbending woman who had so determinedly locked me out of her life. She wasn't strong any more, all her fight was gone.

Something happened when I arrived that morning. Her face lit up when she saw me in the doorway; for a few seconds the pain let go its vice-like grip and she was completely transformed by joy. She said '*Tu agai ya* . . .' 'You're here . . .' I was so surprised that I looked over my shoulder to see who was coming in behind me, but there wasn't anybody there. Her smile was for me.

I can put my hand on my heart and say that was the first time in my entire life I felt my mum was pleased to see me. It made me incredibly happy. I wanted to go over and hold her tight and tell her I loved her, but I knew that if she didn't respond I'd be really upset. So I just said, 'Yeah, I'm here, Mum.' And I got my chair and sat next to her, very casually.

I'd like to be able to say that I behaved differently, that I showed her all the love that she'd spent years rejecting, but I wasn't brave enough. The moment was too nice and I didn't want to lose it. There she was in her chair and the sun was shining through the window on her and she was genuinely pleased to see me. I'll have that picture in my mind for the rest of my life.

I kept going to see her during the few days that were left, and Mum started to show me a side of her that was human and compassionate, a side I'd never seen before. She'd always been so strict about her position, who she was and what she said, but now she knew she was dying she let her guard down. When I went there now, it was just her and me, and I could sit there, holding her hand.

I wanted to ask her all those same questions, 'Mum, what do you really feel about me, and how you treated me? Do you feel bad about Robina and what happened to her?' I know that sounds selfish because she was dying, but I still had these unanswered questions buzzing round my head. For years I'd been waiting and hoping for a proper reconciliation, and now time had cheated us. I couldn't ask her anything important. She was just a frail old lady preparing to die. But there was one change. In those last days I came to believe that she was proud of me. She didn't verbalize it, but I think she felt it. I hope she did.

The nurses warned me the day she was going to die. I'd been there about an hour and she'd been quiet and peaceful, but then she started trying to tell me something. Her voice was barely a whisper, so I bent down really close to her mouth and through her ragged breath I could just make out the words, 'Balbir, Ginda, go . . .' With her dying breath she was asking me to make way for my siblings but this time, knowing it would be the last time, I said, 'I'm not going, Mum,' and I think she was okay about it because she squeezed my hand and seemed to relax.

In the next hour or so they all arrived, Dad – looking utterly worn and dejected – Prakash, Ginda, Yasmin, Balbir, Lucy . . . We were all of us crammed into that tiny room, pressed together, peering at the fragile figure of our mum as, breath by painful breath, she let go of her life. I was closest to her, at the top of the bed, when she died. I was holding her hand and Balbir was hissing at me to let go of it and move over but I wouldn't. She knew what was happening and she was moaning, 'No, no . . .'

You could almost see the cancer travelling through her; her body twisted and twitched. Her mouth was so dry that I kept wetting her lips with a little sponge. Tears were pouring down my face. Everyone was crying, and every so often one of the sisters would call out, 'Mum . . .'

And then at the end she suddenly said, 'Robina, I'm coming to you,' and her hand went limp.

Later, when all the formalities had been dealt with, I drove myself home. The others didn't even say goodbye to me. I think they all went home with Dad. I've never felt so alone, before or since.

20

I made it my business to keep my eye on Dad and Sunny after Mum died. Dad needed help with him. There he was in his retirement being mother, father and now both grandparents to that little kid. And Sunny was a handful. I did the school stuff, talking to the teachers and going to parents' evenings, but I also tried to visit them in Dale Road quite regularly. My life had a pattern by then. A couple of months after Mum died Raj and I got married, in a registry office without any fuss. He was working in the garage, I was teaching aerobics, it was easy to find the time to go to Dale Road but it was the same old thing: Dad couldn't admit that he was seeing me, I could never go there without ringing first. I still minded that. Try as I might, we never recovered our old closeness; he kept an invisible barrier between us, almost as if he was afraid.

I arrived at his house one day to find Sunny sulking in front of the telly and Dad fretting about money. 'He says he has to have this brand of trainers and I don't know how I can afford them, Jasvinder. You know, they cost forty pounds.'

'Don't buy them for him, Dad. He's a kid. He just needs something to wear playing football.'

'He says all his friends have this kind. And your mother would have bought them for him, I know that. She always made sure he had the best.'

Dad wanted the best for him too, he doted on that boy. I once found them play-wrestling in the living-room. I was so surprised; I'd never seen Dad doing anything so undignified in my life. 'You can't let the young ones win all the time,' he said, smiling to cover his embarrassment as, breathing heavily, he collapsed onto a chair.

I wonder if my siblings resented the fact that Dad was there for Sunny in a way he'd never been for us. I didn't mind, until he took Sunny back to his village, Kang Sabhu, to meet the family – something all the others had already done with Mum. I wasn't jealous but I wished that I could go. The stories Dad told me about that place were still so clear in my mind. All the time they were away I was wondering what Dad's reunion with his family would be like. He told me when he got back that everyone in the village came out to meet them, they had a great feast and endless celebrations. It took me weeks to pluck up the courage but one day, when we were sitting together drinking tea, I did blurt out the question.

'Will you take me with you to India one day, Dad? I want to meet Bachanu. I'd love to see the farm, all the places that you used to tell me about.'

Dad's hand trembled slightly as he lowered his cup into its saucer, but he looked me straight in the eye as he said, 'Shame travels, Jasvinder. If you visited my family you would taint them with your disgrace. I will not be party to that.'

Going about my business I noticed a drop-in women's centre in the middle of town and it set me thinking about what I might do to help other women like my mum. I was haunted by the last weeks of her life. I kept having this vision of her in her hospital bed, fading away, stubbornly refusing to eat the food on offer because it wasn't Asian; surrounded by people talking too loudly in a language she'd heard for years but couldn't understand. All her years in Derby she'd buried herself in the Asian community and then, right at the end, she'd been plucked out of her little enclave and left like a snail without its shell, pitifully vulnerable and exposed.

That stuck with me. It lodged in my mind with the same insistent tick as Robina's death had done. If Robina had only ignored the strictures of the community she relied on to protect her; if she could just have found the courage to reach out and embrace the culture of the country she was born in, she needn't have died. The tragedy of that possessed me. I could feel the sorrow and anger fermenting inside me, build-ing an energy that propelled me towards action. I felt I owed it to Robina to do something constructive with my life and, more than that, I wanted to do something to change the world that had failed my family. A small part of me, fuelled by bitterness, also wanted to show Balbir and my sisters that I didn't need them. I'd felt so totally alone driving away from Mum's deathbed. If they didn't want me I would prove to them that I could tread my own path and still make some-thing of myself.

On the way home from a class one day I stopped at the women's centre. It was in a big old Victorian building and the actual centre was one big room with two or three offices and a tiny little kitchen off it. It was all pretty shabby but the atmo-sphere was friendly. It was easy to feel relaxed.

I was buying myself a cup of tea when the woman standing

beside me stirring sugar into her cup said, 'I haven't seen you here before. Were you after anything in particular?'

She was a white woman, large and jolly-looking, with something comforting about her. I explained that I'd come because I wanted to help other people. 'I wondered if you needed any volunteers?'

'Always,' she said, taking me by the elbow and steering me into a tiny, cluttered office where, having swept a chair clear of papers, she sat me down and asked me about myself. She was quite brief and businesslike and I just gave her the bare details before she said, 'At the moment we're badly in need of volunteers in our pregnancy testing centre. There's a slot on Saturday mornings if you'd be interested.'

I agreed to that. She said I'd be shadowing someone else to start with but as soon as I was ready I could do the Saturday session on my own. She wrote my name down in the register of volunteers and then, before she said goodbye, she introduced herself as Trish.

The following Saturday I was back at the women's centre at 9 a.m. The actual process I had to learn was easy. You opened up the centre, got all the glass slides, droppers and pipettes organized and, by the time you were ready to start, there was usually a queue of women in the waiting-room. I sometimes saw as many as fifteen in one two-hour session. They'd come in, one by one, clutching their urine sample, and you had to ask the date of their last period. The test was easy, it just took a couple of minutes and we did it while they were sitting there. The interesting bit came when you had to cope with their reactions.

I remember one woman, I'd say she was about forty, and she was very quiet and still. I looked up at her as we waited to see if the 'positive' circle would appear on the slide and she was biting her lip; she looked so apprehensive. She was pregnant and when I told her so, she went bright red and tears spouted from her eyes. 'I don't believe it,' she kept saying.

I stretched out my hand to touch hers. 'I'm so sorry . . .' But she interrupted me.

'No, don't be sorry. I'm thrilled, really. It's just the shock. I've been trying for so long that I'd given up hope. I didn't tell my husband I was coming here today because I didn't want to disappoint him. Are you really *sure* it's positive?'

But of course there were women who were devastated. Young women who dreaded telling their parents. Married women appalled to find they were carrying babies conceived while their husbands were working away. Tired women exhausted by the prospect of a sixth or seventh pregnancy. We gave them all a confirmation slip to give to their doctor and we gave those who wanted it information about abortion. We supported them all, whatever their choices, and I could see they valued that support. It made me realize that there *were* women out there that I could help.

21

The one thing an aerobics teacher has to do is smile. No matter what's going on in your life, however down you feel, when you step out in front of that class you plaster a smile on your face and you don't let it slip until the last woman has left at the end of your hour. I came to value that. With a false grin on my face I could almost convince myself that I was all right.

Raj and I were teaching some of my classes together by then. He'd trained as an aerobics teacher not long after we started our relationship. We must have looked like the golden couple in our big smiles and our sports gear. And we did have our moments. He could be funny, charming and attentive and when he was I loved him. I wanted so much to love him and I tried really hard to please him. But from the start of our marriage it wasn't easy.

I lay awake at night thinking about my future. I needed qualifications. I'd left school twelve years earlier with nothing, I was completely ill-equipped for independent life and I wanted to change that. The thought of studying again was scary, but I made up my mind to do it. I knew there was a college on

Kedelston Road and on the way to work one day I parked outside it.

It was a big place, much bigger than I'd expected, with a sweeping lawn leading up to the main building. I didn't know how I was going to find what I wanted. There were students milling about, but they all looked so sure of themselves and confident that I didn't dare ask any of them. I pushed through the swing doors and kept going until I found a desk marked RECEPTION.

'Hello,' I said. 'I've come to enquire about doing my A levels here.'

There was a middle-aged woman sitting behind the desk and she smiled at me as she said, 'You're in the wrong place, I'm afraid, my dear. We don't do A levels here, this is a university.'

She said it kindly, but I felt such an idiot. I thought she would think me so above myself, so ignorant not even being able to recognize a university.

'I'm, I'm, I'm sorry,' I stammered. 'I thought . . .'

But I couldn't stay to get the words out. I turned and fled, running blindly back through the building, out of its swing doors and onto the grass where the air felt cool against my burning cheeks. I didn't stop running until I reached my car which I leapt into hoping it would swallow me up and hide my humiliation.

'Sorry, my dear, this is a *university*.' Those words rang in my ears until my exercise class started and the Madonna tape drowned them out.

I didn't give up though. I found Derby Tertiary College in Wilmorton in the phone book and discovered they held adult education classes in a special block at our local infant school. I signed up to do an A level in English language and literature. I didn't mention it to Raj until it was all sorted out, but when I did he said, 'That's a good idea. I think I'll do that too.'

Going back to school felt so strange. All that red brick, the lino on the floor, the funny mixed-up smell of chalk and polish. There were about ten in the class, different sorts of people but all of them like me, wanting to better themselves. We looked big and uncomfortable wedged in behind the wooden desks.

The first book we read was Maya Angelou's *I Know Why the Caged Bird Sings*. I loved reading that. To be honest with you, I'd hardly opened a book in the twelve years since I'd left school and I'd forgotten what it's like to lose yourself in someone else's world, to be so hungry to know what's on the next page that you can't get your eyes across the words quick enough. That woman's courage took my breath away. I could so identify with her feelings of abandonment and isolation it was like she was speaking right to me.

In the class discussions there was so much I wanted to say. Our teacher encouraged everyone to chip in. 'Let's think about Maya's sense of displacement. Does it make her vulnerable to Mr Freeman's sexual advances? Does anybody have a view on that? Anybody want to start the ball rolling?'

My hand shot up, and I jumped right in almost before the teacher had acknowledged me, but I'd hardly started when I heard this derisive snort. It was Raj, who was sitting right beside me. I stopped and looked at him. The teacher looked too. 'Wait your turn, Raj,' he said. 'Let Jasvinder finish.'

'Yeah, sure, sorry. It was just the way she said . . .' He was making out that he was having to suppress his laughter. 'The way she said . . . oh, never mind, forget it. You go on, sorry, Jas.'

I found it really hard to pick up my thread. My thoughts had got all muddled and I'd lost confidence in them anyway. I stammered out a couple of sentences and then shut up. I didn't put my hand up much after that.

But Raj couldn't kill the pleasure I found in reading. Books opened up a whole new world for me. I joined the local library and plundered the biography section as often as I could: I found inspiration reading other women's stories. Writing essays was the hard part, it was so long since I'd had to use my brain that way. Sometimes I struggled to marshal my jumble of thoughts into orderly paragraphs but I was determined to stick with it. At school it had sometimes seemed so pointless: my sisters had all left aged sixteen to get married and then go on to factory work. Why should I be any different? But now the fact that I was working towards a qualification, something that would empower me, made me feel strong. For the first time in my life I had a sense of purpose and it was strengthened when, one spring morning at the women's centre, with my period five days late, I did my own pregnancy test. As I sat there watching the slide develop I weighed the thrill of new life against my stormy marriage. I didn't know what to feel as I saw the thin blue line begin to emerge confirming that I was pregnant. As I watched it growing darker and stronger I still felt uncertain. Later, it was Raj's amazed, unaffected delight – 'We're going to have a baby? You're serious? That's wonderful!' – that made my mind up for me. Perhaps a new life would mean a new beginning for us.

In my last term of doing A levels the tutor talked to us about our options for the future. He asked if I'd thought of doing a degree and told me about an open day at the university. My aspirations hadn't climbed that high when I started the course, but he said it was possible, so with Raj and a couple of others, I went to have a look.

*   *   *

I was drawn to the Social Sciences building and I found the tutors there full of information and advice. They asked what I wanted the degree for, if I had a particular career in mind, and I told them a bit about my desire to help women. An idea had been slowly formulating in my mind to start a project for women with language and cultural barriers. They told me about various options including Cultural and Social Studies, which I liked the sound of because it gave you the chance to study lots of different subjects. The grades I'd need to get accepted seemed attainable and I decided to make that my goal. I was pleased to have something tangible to aim for.

When the results came Raj and I had both done well enough to go on to university. I remember clutching the slip of paper that had my results on and thinking 'Yes!' I'd got my foot on the ladder that was going to take me to a better place. That night I cooked lots of different dishes and we had an Asian feast; when it was all ready I put on a sari in honour of the occasion. Lisa was there and for once the three of us were happy. It was a real celebration.

I went on with my exercise classes right through my pregnancy, heaving my swollen belly through all the routines. Each week Raj and I did a couple of classes together and I was glad of the break our double act gave me. I'd lead a set of exercises, then slow down while he led one, and so it went. I made the bump work for me, though. 'If I can do it with a belly like this, you've no excuse! Come on!' It made the women laugh and try that little bit harder.

I was meant to take a class the day Maria was born. I waved at Raj as I drove off that morning and called through the window, 'See you later.' My first appointment was at the dentist's for a check-up. His rooms were up a couple of flights of stairs and I remember using the handrail to haul myself up. I was still eight weeks from my due date, but I felt hot and heavy as I flopped into his chair. The dentist has never held any terrors for me, and I was relaxed as he clipped on the paper bib, wound back the chair and started to probe my mouth. But suddenly my head started to swim, I felt really dizzy and the room began to blur. I lifted my hand to stop him and I remember struggling to sit up before it all became too difficult and I slid backwards into darkness.

Waking up again was very strange. The first thing I became aware of was the feel of foil against my skin; I was wrapped up like a turkey. I was lying on a trolley which was narrow and enclosed and I felt trapped. I was in pain. Something was covering my nose and mouth and I wanted it off me. I reached up to feel it, to remove it, and felt the sharp tug of an IVF line in my arm. I opened my eyes to find a bank of monitors winking and blinking beside me.

'Don't do that, leave the mask in place.' A nurse appeared beside me; her restraining hand was firm but gentle. 'It's oxygen, you need it. Your lung collapsed while you were on the operating table and you're in intensive care.' Her words drifted through the drugs being pumped into me and suddenly found my brain. Operating table? The fog cleared and I snapped out of it at once.

'Where's my baby? What's happened to my baby?'

The nurse was quick to reassure me. 'You've had a little girl. She's small but she's going to be fine. She's in paediatric ICU and she's in very good hands. That's the very best place for her at the moment.'

'Can I see her? I need to see her.'

The nurse was round and motherly. She bent forward and smoothed the hair from my forehead. 'Not just now. You need to rest. You gave us all a fright. We thought we'd lost you.'

For the next couple of days life drifted in and out of focus. My first clear memory is of someone putting Maria into my arms and telling me she was two days old. She was tiny. She'd weighed less than five pounds but the nurses said she was doing well. For a while she did better than me. I had had an abrupted placenta and lost so much blood they thought I wouldn't make it. The ambulance man who had brought me in came to see me on the ward and told me that on the way to hospital he stuck needles into my feet to try and get a reflex but I didn't have one. He looked really relieved to find me sitting up in bed. Even the dentist sent flowers and a card. He told me at my next appointment that I'd given him such a fright he went home and read up all his childbirth notes.

Raj was thrilled with the baby. He said he didn't mind not having a boy. His parents were disappointed though and they didn't like it that I'd chosen Anna as her second name. His mum explained why: 'You know, Jasvinder, that an *ana* is an Indian coin? A coin so small it is almost worthless. Surely you can't name her after that.'

22

Maria's birth came at a time of change for us. Raj's dad sold the garage and Raj had to sell his house so he could pay off his ex-wife. I came out of hospital with Maria and we spent just a couple of months there before we had to move out. Raj had arranged for us to move over to Nottingham to live with his parents. He said it would just be for a little while, until we found our own place, but I remember packing up my stuff with a sense of dread: I was about to become the dutiful Asian wife, trapped in her in-laws' house. Like any bride whose marriage had been arranged, I would be under constant scrutiny.

I did what I could to fit in and be what they wanted but that wasn't always easy. If I ever asked Raj to help me clear the table or do the washing-up his mother would exclaim: 'I won't have my son washing pots. Not in this house.' I didn't want to disrespect her, so I never spoke above my station. I was very quiet and submissive, I put on my Indian suits when I came indoors and kept to our room when I could. I felt it was them against me.

I was frightened of Raj by then, and I think his mum knew it.

She certainly knew what was going on between us because she witnessed quite a lot of it. She was in the next-door room the night a row blew up about Lisa. I'd made Raj a curry using lots of chillies. I'd gone to real trouble with it because I was trying to please him. It was just for him and me, and we were sitting there eating it when he said, 'Is your daughter coming here tomorrow?'

He knew she was coming; I'd told him so the day before. I felt he was needling me deliberately, like he did when he and his mum talked about Lisa being an untouchable. Something inside me snapped. I dropped the meek, cowed voice I was used to using by then and sneered, 'Don't worry, I'll make sure Lisa is out of your way.'

He didn't like that. It surprised him. He stopped with his fork halfway to his mouth and stared at me, but I brazened it out and stared right back. 'What did you say?' he said, letting the fork fall back onto his plate and pushing his chair back. He stood up and leant over me, eyeballing me. My heart was fluttering in my chest like a trapped bird but I was determined not to let him know that. I eyeballed him back.

'You'll keep her out of my way, will you?' he said and, plunging a hand into the pot of curry sitting on the table, he pulled out a fistful and hurled it at the wall.

As the mess of food slid onto the floor Raj reached for the pot again and I tried to grab it from him. I wanted to stop this before it got out of hand. There was a tug of war over the pot, then Raj suddenly let go. As though in slow motion the remaining curry emptied itself all over me, some of it flying up into my face and eyes. I heard myself gasp with the pain. I was so shocked that I just sat there, with the food dripping off me. I heard a hiss as Raj unscrewed the bottle of lemonade that had been on the table. For one confused moment I thought he was getting me a drink. But he poured it over me, all of it. It ran down my face through all the curry and, despite the shock, I can remember thinking what a weird taste it had as it trickled into my mouth.

I was coughing and spluttering, squeezing my eyes tight shut against the pain. Rats' tails of hair stuck to my face and my Indian suit was plastered tight across my body. When eventually I felt that it was safe to open my eyes, I realised that Raj was just standing there staring at me. I got a cloth from the sink and started clearing up. "Don't bother doing that," he said and his voice wasn't bullying any more. If anything, it was embarrassed.

I went on mopping up the mess and then his mum came in, in through the door that had been open all that time. There is no way that she hadn't heard everything and – if she was sitting in her usual chair – probably seen quite a bit too, but she was all bright innocence. 'Oh dear, what happened here?'

Fifteen minutes later when I had showered and put clean clothes on, Raj appeared at our bedroom door. 'You shouldn't have bothered to change,' he smiled. 'You looked quite sexy wet.'

Looking back, I can't believe I was so passive. He could be as kind as you like and for a long time I believed that the way I behaved affected that. I craved his kindness. I did all I could to earn it, I was so desperate to make a success of my second marriage. I thought I would never be able to hold up my head in Derby if my family knew I'd failed again.

When Raj was nice it was like the sun had come out and I felt I could do anything. I'd clung to my vision of a project for women with language and cultural barriers and he always backed me on that. I'd done my research and found there was nothing like it in Derby. Down at the women's centre I mentioned it to Trish.

'If I were you I'd do the Listening Skills Course at the Rape Crisis Centre over the road,' she advised me. 'If you are going to do any sort of befriending that would really help.' She took me into the office and rummaged about in a big grey filing cabinet until she found an application form. 'There's a new course starting in a couple of weeks' time. See if they'll take you on that.'

I had no idea what to expect when I turned up to the first session. The Rape Crisis centre was in an office building but the room we used had been made to seem cosy with soft lighting and candles. Cushions and low chairs had been arranged in a circle. Two trained counsellors were running the course, Sylvia, who was about my age, mid to late twenties, and Glenda, who I should think was ten years older. They were both lovely, calm, peaceful people. There were eight of us students, all sorts aged from twenty up to about fifty, but I was the only Asian woman there.

The first part of the course was about revelation and self-discovery. For two sessions I listened, fascinated, as the other women told horrific stories about their lives and the horrors were absorbed by the rest of the group. There were stories of rape, abuse, violence and depression all coming out of women who looked so together, so on top of their lives. I couldn't believe they were spilling their shame to a group of strangers. I could see by the way their bodies relaxed when they'd finished speaking that it was like letting out poison, but I couldn't do it myself. Such openness was completely alien to me. It was like a foreign language.

Then week three came and Glenda said she was going to divide us into pairs so we could take it in turns to be speaker and listener. It was an exercise in empathetic, active listening. I was to do it with Alicia and we were to speak from personal experience.

Alicia spoke first. We sat opposite each other and she was telling me all these terrible things that had been done to her when she was young. I was listening and practising all the things we'd been told about: empathy, repeating stuff back, being non-judgemental, providing reassurance. I was practising what we'd learnt but at the same time I was getting really sucked into her story. I'd never talked to anyone like this before. Because it was one to one it was just so intimate.

Then it was my turn. At that point in the course I hadn't told a single secret thing about myself. It had just been the barest bones: I was married, I had two daughters, one of them lived with my ex-husband, I taught keep-fit. I hadn't planned what I was going to say now, but suddenly I found myself talking about Robina. I'd never told anyone, even Raj didn't know the details, but I told Alicia everything: how Robina was forced to marry a stranger when she was fifteen, how she ended up on her own with a tiny baby, how her marriage was so unhappy, how Mum wouldn't help her, nor Dad, nor the community leader, how she felt so frightened and alone that finally she burnt herself to death. I even told her about Mum not wanting me at the mourning.

I was looking at Alicia's face all the time I was talking. I'd thought at first I'd feel ashamed but I wasn't, I felt I was vindicating Robina. Alicia wasn't doing the reassurance or the repeating back, she was just looking horrified, her face was sort of crumbling, and when finally I stopped talking she threw her arms around me and burst into tears. 'I understand, I understand,' she started, but I stopped her.

'You don't understand, don't say that.' I was crying now and having opened my heart all my pent-up grief and rage were spilling out of it onto poor Alicia. 'How could you understand what it's like to ask for help and have your mother turn her back on you. Your mother! The person you rely on to love you and protect you. Don't say you understand that because unless it's happened to you, you couldn't understand, you don't.'

That session marked a turning point for me. It violated so many of the premises on which my whole life had been built. Mum's insistence on preserving the family's good name and presenting a good face meant anything unpleasant had always been buried within the confines of our family. The concept of trusting an 'outsider' to listen sympathetically and not to judge you was never even mooted. Secrecy was a cornerstone of my childhood. Now I'd cracked that cornerstone and, to my amazement, the world was still turning just the same.

I'd told the truth about something bad that had happened, I'd exposed some of my deepest, ugliest feelings and they'd been accepted. I wasn't judged or criticized, made to feel ashamed or scorned. I was believed and – more important – I was valued. Those women's empathy showed me that my experience wasn't shameful or disgraceful. It was part of me and it made me who I was. I sat there that evening and it was as if my eyes had been opened. I looked back at my childhood and realized that the web of secrecy Mum spun around us had made me blind to so many good things in the world, things like truth and honesty and compassion.

As for Alicia, she became and still is a valued friend. Over the years she has taught me such a lot about unconditional love.

I participated in the course after that, as fully as I could. In addition to the group sessions you had to have an hour each week with one of the counsellors. I saw Glenda. We talked about the feelings the listening course was bringing up in us and mine were monumental. All the stuff I'd suppressed for so long came tumbling out. My sessions with Glenda released a torrent of emotion and with it came a flood of angry questions. Why did Mum maintain that unhappiness was just a normal part of married life? Why did she not protect her daughters? Why did she treat us like puppets rather than autonomous individuals? Couldn't she see we had a right to choice, to our own fulfilling lives?

Glenda suggested I go into counselling. She said I needed help. At first I was reluctant, but as my inner turmoil grew I agreed to it, breaking another childhood taboo. Sylvia agreed to be my counsellor. She saw me every week for about a year and she never charged me for it. She did that from the kindness of her heart. I didn't tell anybody about it, not even Raj; as far as he was concerned I was still doing a course. I told Sylvia everything. Week after week she sat there listening to me sobbing as I poured out the sorry details of my life. The knowledge that I could trust her with that was so important to me, but a question played in my mind and one day I asked her, 'Sylvia, how can you listen to all this? How can you take on all this sadness and still carry on with your life?'

She smiled and said, 'Don't you worry about that.'

She was the most giving person and she became someone I knew I could always turn to. She died of cancer five years ago and I miss her still.

23

While I was doing the listening skills course I started talking to people about my idea for helping women with cultural and language barriers and the more I talked the more real it became to me. People gave me good advice, some offered to help. It was one of the women from the course who told me to get in touch with the Council for Voluntary Service and that's how I met Wendy Lloyd, who became my mentor. I went to her with a storm of ideas about how I wanted to help women and she gave me facts. She told me if I ever wanted to access any funding I'd need a constitution setting out my aims and objectives, and a management committee with at least four members. She was so supportive; she even helped me find the perfect name for my project: Karma Nirvana. From the whirlwind of ideas I threw out at her she had homed in on the important things: peace of mind and enlightenment.

We needed a proper base. 'Well, the Rape Crisis lot used to use the little room at the back. Maybe you could have that,' said Trish when I bumped into her at the women's centre.

204   *Jasvinder Sanghera*

'But I can't afford to pay rent, we haven't got any money,' I said.

She shrugged and smiled encouragingly. 'Ask if you can have it for free then. It's sitting there empty. Why not give the management a presentation then ask them. You've nothing to lose.'

I'd never heard the word 'presentation'; I had no idea what it was but Trish said all I had to do was talk about my plans with the same passion I'd shown her. She said it would be easy and once she'd persuaded me to do it, she put me on the agenda for the next management committee meeting. I was item number four.

The day came and I was so nervous. I paced up and down outside the meeting room waiting for my turn to come. Each minute seemed to last for ever and as time ticked by I could feel my confidence draining away. I hadn't got a presentation, I hadn't got any facts or figures, I hadn't even got any notes. All I had was my dream and how could I sell that?

Eventually I was called in. What actually happened in there is a bit of a blur. Somebody asked me to take a seat and I heard myself saying that if they didn't mind I'd rather stand. I felt hot and my mouth was very dry. I took a deep breath.

'I've got this idea, well, a vision really, of a project that would help women who are facing language and cultural barriers. I can't say exactly what that help would be because I haven't really started yet, but I know there are women out there who have got problems and who do need help. I first thought of it because of my mum, who died two years ago. She'd lived here almost all her life, but she never learnt English and when she was in hospital . . .'

Once I'd started the words seemed to fly out of me. I'd worried that I would be tongue-tied and forget what I wanted to say but once I got onto Mum it all came pouring out. I wanted them to see her as I did, a little old lady who'd worked hard all her life and paid her taxes and then, at the end, been let down by the people looking after her. I explained that she'd been hurt and humiliated because those paid to care for her didn't understand her needs.

My heart was racing, I felt like I was talking at a hundred miles an hour, and I could feel my hands dancing all over the place, but they seemed to be helping me to talk and so I didn't try to keep them still, I just went with it. I still do that today. If you made me keep my hands behind my back I'd be a mute.

When I'd explained about Mum, I told them about Robina, her awful suffering and how her agonizing death had happened because she didn't know where to turn for help. I shared with them the thought that was lodged like a thorn in my conscience: that a kind word or a sympathetic ear might have saved Robina's life. And then – I couldn't really believe I was doing this – I told them about me. I could never have done that before the listening skills course but the trust I'd found there gave me the confidence. Glenda, Sylvia, Alicia and the others had brought me to a place where I could look those women in the eye and tell them how I'd run away to escape a forced marriage and how I'd had to survive without my family ever since.

'I've had nowhere to turn for help, so you see, I know from personal experience that a project like mine is needed. I know there are other women like me and my mum and Robina. I see them every day in Derby, scuttling about like shadows, with their eyes on the ground. I know I could help those women, so I'm asking you now, please help me realize my dream.'

I stopped there, slightly breathless, and for a moment every-one in the room was quiet. The woman who broke the silence said: 'I think you're very brave,' and that really surprised me. Then several of them spoke at once and they were saying things like 'How can we help you?' and 'What do you see yourself doing?' and 'What will you need?'

'What I need is a room, a base for the project. Which is called Karma Nirvana, by the way, I think I forgot to tell you that. I wouldn't be able to pay for a room at the moment, but I'd pay when I could. This would be a good place for the project because so many women come here anyway. Some of those women must have issues I could help with, and you could tell them that I exist.'

'And what would you be offering them exactly?'

'To be honest with you, I can't say exactly because I've got nothing to offer at the moment. I need to build up resources. But I envisage giving support, both emotional and practical, infor-mation and advice . . . I want to meet the needs that I'm presented with.'

The chairwoman rang next morning. They'd all been im-pressed by my passion, and I could move in as soon as they'd had the carpets cleaned. I was so pleased that I could hardly take it in. I had been so convinced that they were going to turn me down.

I collected the keys about a week later. It was a huge room, with a really big window that let in loads of light. It looked right onto the Rape Crisis Centre's office and that was an important link for me. There was nothing in it except the desk and the chair which were pushed into one corner, but I stood there in the middle of the empty space and thought, 'This is mine and it's going to be special. I'm going to shape this and put my mark on it and achieve something for every woman who walks through that door. That's my dream and I'm going to make it real.'

24

I always knew that the best way to spread the word about Karma Nirvana would be through the exercise classes. Not the ones I did with Raj, in the leisure centre. Those were popular, but the ones that really mattered to me – and the ones I knew would be important to Karma Nirvana – were the ones I held in community centres in areas of social deprivation, areas like the one where I'd grown up.

It was mostly Asian women who came to those classes, and I knew for some it was the only proper outing they had in a week. Their husbands let them come because they knew they wouldn't meet any men there and because they could bring their kids. I didn't mind as long as the kids played quietly at the back of the hall; Maria was often there, sucking on her thumb as she slept in her car seat, and I sometimes brought Lisa. To make the women feel more comfortable I used to black out the windows with sheets of cardboard before every class. I renamed them the Karma Nirvana classes; I made sure everyone who came knew about the project and it wasn't long before women started approaching me, wanting advice.

I had a few who wore flashy leotards, but most of them chose to exercise in their Indian suits, which was fine by me as long as they wore trainers. Some of them had husbands who insisted on it; others were just conditioned to it. There was one girl who stood out because she wore a shapeless old tracksuit which was so worn and hideous that I could only think she wanted to make herself look plain. Everything about her spoke of loneliness: she used to stick herself firmly in the back row and she never made eye contact. I wanted to talk to her about Karma Nirvana but before I got around to it, she approached me at the end of one class.

'Do you teach anywhere else?' she said, her eyes still glued to the floor.

'At the leisure centre on Mondays but I do Thursdays here as well.'

'I see. Thanks.' She started to turn away when I caught her arm and asked if she would like to get a coffee. 'I'm starting up a project that might interest you. I'd like to tell you about it, if you've time.'

Her name was Ayesha. We went to a café just down the road and stayed for about half an hour. I don't think she looked directly at me in all that time. I told her about Karma Nirvana and she seemed interested, but there was something absent about her, as though a big part of her was locked away. I got the impression she was weighed down by a secret she was keeping really close to her chest. I did learn that things hadn't worked out for her at home and she was living on her own. I resolved to look out for her, to persuade her to talk to me again.

'I really feel I'm getting somewhere now, like Karma Nirvana is actually coming together,' I said to Ayesha the third or fourth time we had coffee together after class. It had become a bit of a habit and she always hung back at the end of the hour, as if she was hoping I'd ask.

We always went to the same place, and we usually sat at the same Formica-topped table, right at the back where we could be peaceful. That was important because Ayesha spoke so quietly that I really had to strain to hear what she said. Not that she said much; mostly she just answered my questions as briefly as she could. When I told her about Karma Nirvana she murmured, 'That's good, you must be pleased.' I felt like I was trying to reach her through a pane of glass.

Suddenly I had a thought. I didn't question it, I just opened my mouth and said, 'Ayesha, did I tell you why I started Karma Nirvana?'

Eyes glued to the table, she shook her head. So I told her about Robina and me, and how even now my family wouldn't have anything to do with me. She didn't look at me while I was talking but she was so still and alert that I knew she was listening. 'That's why I'm doing it, Ayesha, because all these years I've felt so lonely and ashamed and I know, I just know, there must be so many other women like me.'

Ayesha had been fiddling with a paper serviette, folding and unfolding it, and when I said that last bit her movements became more frantic, she was almost shredding it. Her head was down and I saw a tear splash onto the table. She wiped her cheek with the back of her hand and I thought I heard a whisper. I craned right forward.

'When I was eight, my oldest brother raped me.' She quickly dragged her breath back in, to catch a sob. 'My uncle did it too. For years they went on doing it, sometimes every week. They did it to me over and . . .' She buried her face in her hands and turned towards the wall, her shoulders heaving with sobs.

What could I say to her? *Eight* . . . Younger than my precious Lisa, who was still quite unaware of the beauty of her firm, round, innocent body. If any man touched Lisa I knew I would kill him. But Ayesha's mother did nothing to protect her daughter; in fact I discovered later that she'd connived in the abuse.

Ayesha didn't tell me any more just then. I gave her Karma Nirvana's number and told her that if ever she rang it I'd get back to her as soon as I could. And she did ring, often. She kept coming to the classes, but I saw her at other times as well and I gradually learnt the full story of her suffering. She told me how as a child, sore and terrified, she'd plucked up the courage to say what her brother and her uncle had been doing. 'My mum slapped my face. She said, "Don't you dare disgrace this family. Cry at the bottom of the garden if you must, but don't bring your fuss in here." My brother must have known she said that, because he stopped being careful, he did it more and more.'

Aged sixteen, Ayesha was sent to Pakistan to get married. She was told she was going on a family holiday. I wasn't surprised to hear that, as a wife, she swapped one sort of abuse for another. Her husband wasn't much older than her, but he was hefty and bad-tempered. After one particularly violent assault she went sobbing to her mother who told her – again – to be mindful of the family name and stop complaining.

Those words struck me like a dart that went right through me and carried me back down the years to where I sat, watching my older sisters beg for my mother's sympathy. 'Not a word of this to anyone. It's a private matter for our family.' That's what Mum used to say as Dad drove us home after those terrible sessions. Now, for the first time ever, I realized that many, many of the Asian families we knew probably shared that same secret Mum was desperate to keep. It wasn't just us.

'I couldn't take it after that, Jas. I ran away,' Ayesha told me with the tears pouring down her face. We were sitting on the scratchy grey carpet tiles in my room, Karma Nirvana's office. I'd yet to get a second chair. 'I haven't seen them since, not Mum, Dad, not anyone. It's been eighteen months and they won't even speak to me on the phone.' I was holding her and she was spluttering through her sobs. We sat together in silence for a long time and when her thin shoulders had almost stopped heaving, she said really quietly, 'It's my little brother I miss most, Jas. And they've told him I'm dead.'

I know my listening to Ayesha helped her. She told me it did and, anyway, I could tell just by looking at her. As the weeks went by she stopped carrying herself like a whipped dog. She said that hearing my story, knowing she wasn't the only one, made her feel stronger. I knew she wasn't ready to make the mental break from her family that I'd made. She was a long way from that. But I tried to nudge her towards seeing things differently. 'You wouldn't treat your worst enemy like you've been treated, would you? You don't have to put up with it, you know, just because the person doing it's your mum.'

I helped Ayesha but also she helped me. I hadn't expected that, but it's true. Her story – which spoke so clearly of cruelty, denial and disownment – clarified my own experience and made me see with absolute certainty that I'd been the victim not the perpetrator of a crime.

That made me feel stronger and so did the knowledge that I was doing something good. What's more, being there for Ayesha helped me rise above my own problems. Raj's treatment of me was increasingly unpredictable. I'd chosen him, I knew I had to stay with him, but I felt I was walking on quicksand whenever I was near him.

Raj was constantly finding fault. It felt like I couldn't do anything right. When I angered him he'd bawl me out and then ignore me. He could keep it up for as long as a week and I used to think I'd go insane. I'd follow him about like a lost child, pleading with him to talk to me. I'd kneel down and pray that he would talk to me. I couldn't function unless things were right between us. Being strong for Ayesha was like a rock that I could cling to.

25

In September 1994 I started at Derby University. I shoul-
dered my bag with three new files and a block of A4 paper
in it, and I felt this big grin spreading across my face as I
walked across the grass towards the doors I'd fled through
two years earlier. There were students everywhere, going
about their business in every direction. Most of them walked
in little groups, chatting and laughing, but they didn't faze
me any more. I could hold my head up, I'd earned my place.
At the age of twenty-nine I'd fulfilled my dream and I was
going to college.

Raj started the same day as me, reading law, but he was in a
different building. The first lecture I had was sociology and as I
sat there waiting for it to begin I surveyed the other students.
They all looked so young and carefree. Two girls just along from
me were discussing all the things they were going to do in
Freshers' Week. There was going to be a disco on the Friday and
one of them, the plumper of the two, was fussing about what she
should wear. It made me smile. Friday was going to be Maria's
first day in the university crèche; Raj's mum usually had her

when I was out, but she was busy on Friday. I'd be racing to pick
her up and then dashing across town in time to collect Lisa from
school. I was longing to see Lisa but the weekends she spent with
us were always tense.

It was my responsibilities more than my age that divided me
from the other students. I was always leaving lectures in a hurry,
rushing off the campus to take an exercise class, or to collect
Maria or to do my jobs at Raj's mum's house. She didn't like me
studying at all. She was proud of having a son at university but
she made it clear she didn't know what I was doing there. If ever
she saw me reading one of my textbooks or setting out my paper
and pens ready to write an essay she'd stop me working. She was
clever about it. She'd start talking to me, knowing I wouldn't
dare ignore her conversation. Or she'd find extra little tasks for
me to do. I was in her house, I couldn't stand up to her, but I
didn't have to give in to her. I crept downstairs in the middle of
the night to study at the kitchen table before sneaking back to
bed at dawn.

I had to work hard to keep up with my studies, and there was
Karma Nirvana too. With the help of Wendy Lloyd I was trying
to access funding; at the very least I needed to maintain a
telephone line and she was a genius at finding little pockets
of money, grants I could apply for. As soon as the telephone was
installed I made sure that I went to the office every day to check
for any messages. And I was trying to get the word out; when I
could find the time I rang round hospitals, health centres, police
stations and social services, making them aware of what we did
and how to reach us. Some people could see the point straight
away; the bored response of others made it clear they thought I
was wasting their time.

I wasn't put off but I was more and more convinced that we needed some sort of focus, an event to launch the project. Early in 1995 I hit on the idea of a women's health day. 'Health's relevant to everyone,' I said to Wendy Lloyd. 'It's important to women of all ages, and to their families. And it's unthreatening so the Asian men won't mind their wives coming.' Wendy agreed and she encouraged me to do it. She was always encouraging and I'll be forever grateful to her.

The health day was a long time in the planning. I knew exactly what I wanted: lots of different speakers, stalls displaying information, interpreters so nobody should feel excluded, food, discussion groups . . . I wanted the whole place alive with activity and interest.

The first person I approached was an Asian nurse in the breast care unit of our local hospital. She was flattered and agreed. That was easy, but I had to do a lot of groundwork for the rest. Eventually I got speakers on mental health, depression, nutrition, cervical screening. I was really pleased about the screening because I knew it was something Mum had never done. She was far too embarrassed.

Several of the women I taught got involved. I found Punjabi and Urdu interpreters; one girl designed some flyers and we spent hours pounding the streets of Derby distributing those as widely as we could. Margaret Redfern, our local councillor, agreed to come and talk and, to my amazement, about a month before the scheduled day our local MP, Margaret Beckett, said she would come and open it. I was thrilled.

The night before it happened I was a bag of nerves. I went through my checklist again and again and went to bed exhausted at about midnight. The last thing I said to Raj was, 'What if it doesn't work out? What if no one turns up?' He groaned and rolled over. 'You've left flyers in almost every shop in Derby. Don't worry, it's going to be great.'

He'd agreed to come and help set up in the morning and then disappear before the event started. I'd let it be known that no men could attend the health day; I knew that would be important for some of the Asian women. I didn't want any of them being barred by their husbands from coming.

Next day I was at the hall by eight o'clock. It was the community hall in which I taught aerobics but in the morning light it looked drab and dusty. The room felt stale and airless; in one corner there was a laden ashtray, forgotten at the tail end of some event the night before. I started wrestling with the sash windows, wondering how we were ever going to make this cavernous space look interesting and inviting.

My volunteers arrived in a flurry of noise and bright-coloured Indian suits and we worked hard erecting tables, arranging chairs, pinning up the posters I'd scrounged. Manjit and Nina filled the tea urns and set out all the cups and saucers and shortly after nine o'clock the food arrived: trays of sandwiches, sausage rolls, samosas, cakes and biscuits. Everything had been donated by a local supermarket. When the people manning the information stands arrived with all their bumph and booklets the picture I'd had in my mind began to take on proper shape.

We were ready just before our ten o'clock deadline. Jassey had dropped Lisa off and she was chasing a balloon round between the stalls. She was going to help in the crèche we'd promised to any mothers bringing children. They trickled in at first; by 10.30 there can't have been more than twelve people in the hall and I was starting to panic when there was a sudden influx. They came through the door in a steady stream: old women, young women, women pushing pushchairs and clutching small children. I stood by the door smiling and welcoming people as they flowed past me in a rainbow parade of saris, dresses, jeans, Indian suits and T-shirts. Shibana stood opposite me and we handed out evaluation forms, asking every woman who walked through the door to fill one in before she left the building. Wendy Lloyd had said feedback like that would be invaluable in attracting funding.

Margaret Beckett arrived and complimented me on the turn-out. Before I knew it I was standing beside her on the stage and she was doing the formal opening. She and Margaret Redfern both mentioned Karma Nirvana and the importance of filling in the evaluation forms, and I began to feel I was bobbing along on a wave of support and encouragement.

The day was even better than I'd hoped. The speakers gave clear, interesting talks and they all made themselves available for questions afterwards. The nurse who'd come to talk about cervical screening was surrounded by Asian women. Lots of the older ones were being helped by the interpreters. Submitting to that sort of screening is so alien to Asian culture – a threat to Asian women's modesty and a blow to their men's possessive pride – that I felt really proud to have created an environment in which they felt safe enough to talk about it.

At lunchtime I heard several women discussing what they'd learnt that morning. One said she was going to go home and fetch her mum. The whole place was buzzing – at one stage I'd say the hall was crammed with 250 or 300 people – and yet the atmosphere was so relaxed and easy.

We'd advertised the day from ten until four, and by four-thirty there were just me, Lisa and a handful of volunteers left. When the last chair had been pushed against the wall I was exhausted but I couldn't remember when I'd been so happy. It

Jasvinder Sanghera

was all congratulations and hugging one another. Lisa counted the evaluation forms for me while we were packing up and she said there were 120. I had them clutched in my hand. I was guarding them with my life because I knew they were the key to Karma Nirvana's financial future.

26

After the Women's Health Day Karma Nirvana's phone finally started ringing. I went to the office on the way from college and the light on the answering machine, which had been disappointingly dark all those months I'd been checking it, was blinking furiously. Some of the messages were blank and I worried that those were from women who had plucked up the courage to ring and then been scared off by the electronic voice of the answering machine. Lots of them were from social services departments wanting information about Karma Nirvana. A few were from people enquiring about the classes.

My original idea had been for a project that would help all women, but it soon became clear that it was Asian women who needed Karma Nirvana. Almost all the calls we took concerned Asian women; I was staggered by the number of them. It was as if a box of ugly secrets had been opened; some days it felt like nothing would stop them pouring out. Some of the first stories I heard still stick in my mind today.

There was the key worker from the YMCA who rang to ask my advice about a seventeen-year-old girl in her hostel. 'She arrived here covered in cigarette burns which she says were inflicted by her brother, but she won't report him, even though he and the rest of the family held her prisoner for almost ten months. They locked her door and boarded up her windows because she wouldn't agree to the marriage they wanted. I can't reach her, Jasvinder. It's like she's dead inside, and now I think she's drifting into prostitution.'

There was a social worker who asked me to mediate between a client and her parents. 'I know her through the truant officer; her parents have been keeping her off school. She's fifteen and she's eight months pregnant, but they've not let her have any medical care at all. They're so ashamed of her condition they won't let her out of the house. I'm scared they're going to make her give birth at home, Jasvinder. She says she loves the father and he wants to support her – he's a Derby-born Asian like her – but I can't find him. He's disappeared and his family is saying nothing.'

And there was Maram. Maram was one of the first women to actually turn up at Karma Nirvana's office. She was visibly pregnant and very upset. 'My husband has disowned me. He has thrown me out and I have nowhere to go.' Through her sobs she spoke in Urdu. I later learnt she spoke no English. 'It is my fault, I know that, but I didn't know how to avoid what happened. I wasn't expecting it. I went to my ante-natal appointment and the doctor who saw me was a man. Always before it has been the midwife. He wanted to listen to my baby's heart. I knew my husband wouldn't like him touching me, but I didn't know the words to make him stop.'

I remember making Maram a cup of tea as I wondered what shocked me most, the way her husband had treated her or her belief that she had brought his cruelty on herself. It reminded me of the day I told Dad a man had flashed at me and Robina on the way home from school. My mild-mannered dad was furious and he raged at us: 'You must avoid these situations, do you want to bring dishonour on yourself?'

I rang the social services and asked for their help. The woman I spoke to agreed to find Maram emergency accommodation and came to collect her from the office. I gave Maram a hug before she left and made her promise to keep in touch.

She did. Three days later she rang me and said she was fine. 'I'm back with my husband, he forgave me.'

'Oh, good, that's good news, Maram.' It sounded suspicious to me. In my experience men – and women – motivated by honour don't have sudden changes of heart.

'He gathered the older members of the community in my mother-in-law's house, as many as could fit in and, in front of them, I begged his forgiveness. I went down on my knees and kissed his feet and begged and he forgave me. So you see, Jasvinder, now I am all right.'

Using the women's evaluation forms as back-up I applied for Lottery funding and, several months after the Women's Health Day, we were awarded £125,000 over three years; enough to establish a proper concern. Through the local paper I recruited three staff and a new management committee and as soon as my co-workers were in place I began to focus on forming links with anyone I thought was relevant: the police, GPs, voluntary agencies like Rape Crisis, primary care groups.

The better known Karma Nirvana became the more people dropped in, all wanting as much support, advocacy and advice as we could offer. My co-workers and I began to find it hard to get anything else done. The solution was to institute a weekly surgery when we were all available to talk. It was instantly popular.

I was learning more each day about the task ahead of me. A social worker with a desperate client told me that Asian women brought here as brides have no rights to benefits or legal aid until their status here is authorized. 'They're trapped with the families who brought them into the country,' she said. I realized that I might have to grow beyond Derby and start campaigning on a national level.

27

Towards the end of my second year at university Raj and I were invited to a wedding in Leeds. It was Rachel, a woman I'd become very close to when I lived there. Raj had met her, but he said he didn't want to go. 'And if I don't go, you don't either.' For several days I wheedled and pleaded but he wouldn't shift. It mattered to me that I went and I finally decided to stand up to him. I told him I would go alone.

'Not unless I agree to it, you won't,' he said. It was all about control. He wanted me tiptoeing round him, begging him to let me go. I played along with it but I'd made my mind up, I was going to see Rachel married.

The day came and Lisa and I, dressed in our best, were heading for the front door when he shouted from the bedroom. 'You're to be back at six o'clock. Have you got that? Don't think you can come and go to suit yourself.'

'Okay, Raj. I'll be back by six,' I said, calm as I could. I was determined not to let him get to me.

'You better be, or you and your untouchable daughter can

find yourselves somewhere else to live. I'm warning you, if you're not back by six o'clock, that's it.'

As we drove out of Nottingham Lisa was pale and silent and I knew she was worrying. 'Where will you go if he throws us out? I can go back to Daddy, but where will you go?'

'Don't worry, darling, he doesn't really mean it.' I didn't feel as brave about it as I sounded but I wanted to reassure her.

At the wedding we forgot our worries. It was a white wedding in a lovely little church. Rachel was marrying a rugby player and all his team mates were there forming a guard of honour. She looked so happy and the groom looked just like the cat that got the cream. They stood in the churchyard, posing for photographs, and even though they were laughing and excited they looked so grounded, standing there together hand in hand.

The reception was at the local football ground. There were old friends there, from the markets, and for the first time in months I relaxed. There were other kids for Lisa to play with and she was happy too. It was good to see her laughing; so much of the time she spent with me was shadowed by the bad feeling between her and Raj. I was so caught up with enjoying myself that I forgot the time and when I looked at my watch it was already five o'clock. I couldn't believe I'd been so careless. Nottingham was more than an hour's drive away.

I immediately rang Raj and asked if we could stay a little longer; I wheedled and begged as he liked me to, but he was adamant. 'Be back here by six o'clock or else . . . Don't push me, Jas.'

My heart was really racing then. I pulled Lisa out of a group of girls who were all dancing together and told her we had to leave as fast as possible. She's always been biddable and, bless her, she didn't make a fuss. Having said my goodbyes I took off my high heels and hurried to the car as fast as I could. We were silent all the way, I was concentrating so hard on driving. My knuckles were white from gripping the wheel so tightly, straining to make my poor old car top its maximum speed of 60 miles an hour. The roads were full of Saturday evening traffic, cruising aimlessly, and it seemed to take for ever.

It was twenty past six as I pulled into the street where Raj's parents lived and I could see, almost at once, that I was too late. Raj's mum was standing by the front door, Maria on her hip, and Raj had just marched past her carrying a box of my books which he dumped on the pavement beside a couple of bulging bin bags, one of which had my favourite jumper spilling out of it.

'You stay in the car, darling,' I said to Lisa as I swung into the kerb and leapt out onto the pavement. 'Raj, I'm really sorry. I meant to be back by six, but I forgot the time and the traffic was terrible, I'm so sorry . . .' The words were rushing out of me and I really meant them, I was genuinely sorry and I thought Raj could have told that, but he just looked at me like I was dirt.

'I told you what would happen if you chose to ignore me . . .' He left the sentence hanging in the air as he turned and walked back into the house. I went to follow him but his mum was still standing in the doorway. She shifted a little to bar my way. She was looking so stern and cold.

I lost my nerve. I wanted to defend myself but there was nothing to say. I was helpless against both of them. 'Okay, Bibi-ji, I'll go,' I murmured to Raj's mum. I went to lift Maria out of her arms, but she wheeled away from me. 'The child is staying here. It's what her father wishes.'

I was so shocked I completely forgot about being respectful. I reached round and grabbed Maria under her arms, but Raj's mum held on tight. 'She is staying with her father,' she repeated.

'I'm not leaving without her,' I said, clutching Maria as firmly as I could.

'Rajvinder, come here quickly!' Raj's mum was pulling too.

Out of the corner of my eye I saw a neighbour's front door open. Raj's mum suddenly let go of Maria and I stumbled backwards. In the car Lisa's arms were open, ready for her little sister.

Raj and his mum stood there watching me as I struggled with the sacks of clothes. A couple of jumpers and a top dropped out as I was carrying them to the car. I told myself to walk tall and proud as I went back for them, but I knew I was scuttling like a thief. I rammed the box of books and files onto the back seat. I wanted to check that all my precious work was there, but I didn't dare.

I should have said something to Lisa as I got back in the car, but I didn't trust myself to speak. I was doing all I could to hold my tears back. As I pulled away from the kerb Raj and his mum were still in the doorway, their faces ugly with anger as they watched us drive away.

On the warmth of Lisa's lap Maria's wails juddered into whimpers and those soon stopped too. My daughters sat quiet as mice with frightened eyes and behind them the back seat was piled high with my possessions. My entire life was in that car and I didn't know where to go. My mind flashed back to the day that Jassey and I ran away to Newcastle and for one crazy moment I thought of going to his house. Even after all we'd been through I knew he'd have me back. I also knew that to take that step would be disastrous.

Habit turned me towards Derby and I drove down the A52 with tears pouring down my cheeks. When I'd been desperate to get back to Nottingham the road had seemed so long and slow, but now the miles flashed past. I was trying to think but my brain felt like cotton wool. I kept hearing Mum's warning that if I married Raj I'd end up getting divorced. I should have listened, but I was so used to her working for her own ends that I hadn't taken any notice. That felt like arrogance now.

Writing this more than ten years later, it strikes me that I was driving towards my home town, the place where I was born and brought up and where almost my entire family live, and yet I had nowhere to go. Of course, I could have turned to one of the women who had befriended me: Glenda, Sylvia or Alicia. They had taught me so much about support and sharing; they'd shown me that secrecy is a stifling bond rather than the protective cloak that Mum perceived it as. I should have trusted them, I know that now, but at the time I didn't. I panicked and in my panic I forgot all I'd learnt. I didn't want any one of those kind, wise women to know that once again I'd failed to sustain a relationship, I didn't want them to see me, with all my things in garbage bags, slinking shame-faced through the night.

And so I turned to Narinder, a friend of Raj's who had seen some of what went on between us. Narinder never intervened, never stopped Raj saying the things he did, but once when we were all three out together he waited until Raj left the table – to go to the toilet or to buy drinks at the bar – and then he let me know he sympathized. Narinder had seen me humiliated by my husband; he'd seen me shamed. With him I didn't have much face to save.

When his image popped into my mind, I thought of the tiny terraced house that Raj and I once picked him up from. I wondered if he'd fit us in. Stopped at a traffic light, I looked across at the girls: Maria had fallen asleep and the sight of Lisa's stoic little face made me realize I didn't have an alternative. I couldn't drive around all night.

I knew Narinder was in because I could see his telly flickering in the sitting-room. I knocked – a pathetic, apologetic knock – and then stood waiting. He opened the door and, as his mind registered what his eyes were seeing, I watched his expression change from annoyed to surprised to quizzical. Before he had time to ask me anything I said, 'Raj has thrown us out, me, Maria and Lisa. We've haven't got anywhere to go. Do you think we could stop here a bit?'

He was taken aback, I could see that, although he did his best to hide it. 'Of course you can, come in.' He stepped back to let me pass him in the narrow passage but then remembered. 'The kids, let's get the kids. And have you got bags?'

We hauled my stuff inside and I settled the girls in Narinder's back bedroom. I was glad to see the bed was big enough for three of us; I was so tired that the thought of sleeping on the floor made me ache all over. Narinder didn't ask me what had happened, he didn't make me talk much at all. He just made me a cup of tea and put me in an armchair and made it clear we could stay as long as necessary.

He said it again before he went out next morning and I thanked him. I didn't want to impose, but I still couldn't think straight. My mind was stuck on the fact that my marriage was over. I'd failed again. I couldn't look the world in the face. As if my shame was blazoned all over me I kept the curtains closed and lurked inside Narinder's house until Lisa and Maria became fretful and Lisa begged me to take them to the park.

Maybe that's when Raj saw me driving away from Narinder's house. Maybe it was just that after two days he'd exhausted all the other possibilities. Either way, at six-thirty on Monday evening he was there, hammering at Narinder's front door. The girls were scared, even Narinder looked alarmed. Raj was battering the door, rattling the letterbox and shouting through it, 'I know you're in there, Jas. You can't deceive me any more. Didn't I say you two were seeing each other?'

Narinder and I looked at each other. I told Lisa to take Maria upstairs to play in our room. Narinder opened the door and Raj burst through it shouting about how Narinder and I were having an affair.

'That's rubbish, Raj. You know it is,' I said.

'She needed somewhere to stay, Raj. You know that, mate. You threw her out,' said Narinder.

'So you sided with her! That's great. That's real loyalty from a friend.'

'I'm not siding with anybody, Raj. Don't be ridiculous. I took Jas in because she and the kids needed somewhere to sleep. End of story. What's going on between you and Jas is nothing to do with me.'

'Dead right, it's not. So kick her out.'

'I'm not going to do that, Raj. No decent person would.'

That riled Raj, I could see. He took a deep breath ready for another tirade but I cut in.

'Thanks, Narinder, but I'll go, we'll go. You've been very generous, but you don't have to put up with this and I can't see Raj giving up while I'm still here.'

'No! You won't go.' Narinder was a mild man but he sounded so determined that both Raj and I shut up and stared at him. He walked past us both and opened the front door. 'Look, mate,' he said to Raj. 'Why don't you go home and cool off a bit. There's nothing going on between me and Jas, I promise you that. But nothing's going to get settled while you're so angry. Come back and talk to Jas when you're feeling calmer. In the meantime she and your daughter are safe while they're here.'

That was brave of Narinder. Raj still had his fists clenched. He looked from Narinder to me and back again and I know he wanted to say something that would put him back in the ring but Narinder's calm reason had deflated him. He shrugged his shoulders and stamped out.

I didn't see him again for a couple of weeks but then, just as unexpectedly, he reappeared with a bunch of flowers and asked if he could talk to me. He took me to a restaurant and said he was so sorry, he loved me so much, he was so determined to change. He said that when he thought that he was going to lose me his life had looked so bleak. He did all he could to woo me and I fell for it. I lapped up his false flattery because I wanted it to be true, I wanted a good man who loved me. For years I'd been nobody's daughter and I needed to make up for that: I needed to be somebody's wife.

I made one condition though. I said we had to have our own place. I said I couldn't live with his parents any more, there was no way we could rebuild our relationship with them watching our every move. Raj agreed and that's how we came to Balfour Road.

His dad lent us the money for that house; it cost £13,000 in an area where anything halfway decent cost £23,000 and I wouldn't say we got a bargain. The house was as derelict as our marriage. It was two up, two down with a tiny unfinished bathroom and a little kitchen at the back. The floors were rough concrete except in the living-room where someone had got as far as laying one floorboard which you had to use like a tightrope when you crossed the room. The walls were bare and damp – so damp that mould grew on some of them that winter – and the window frames were the oldest in the world, they howled and shook in the wind. We used to hang blankets and towels over them to try and keep warm.

We first saw it just a few days after our reunion at Narinder's when we were still floating on a cloud of new hope and romance. I didn't see a wreck, I saw an opportunity and a project that would pull us together. I imagined it painted in pretty colours with fresh curtains at the windows and the dank yard outside transformed into a sunny patio. We'd barely moved in before those hopes were dashed.

When we were scrabbling round for furniture Narinder gave us an old sofa. It had a split in the seat with foam bulging out of it but it was usable. Within weeks of moving into Balfour Road I found myself sitting on that sofa night after night, with my course books open on my lap, wondering where Raj was. 'I've been giving classes, it's going really well for me at the moment' or 'I've been at the gym, if you're going to teach keep-fit you've got to look the part'. Those were the excuses he gave when he came home late and I wanted to believe him.

Often he came home at 2 or 3 a.m. About four hours after he'd crawled into our bed I'd climb out of it to get Maria ready before I began the round of dropping her at nursery, stopping to do my stint at Karma Nirvana and then going on to university. When I came back in the evenings Raj would be gone and the massive roll of lino that you had to dodge round to get up or down the stairs would still be there, untouched, with the box of tools lying unopened beside it. The home-making never happened.

28

Balfour Road is in the heart of the Asian area and I knew I'd bump into my sisters sooner or later. Since Mum died we'd had no contact. I still saw a lot of Dad and Sunny. I was always being called round to talk to Sunny because he was in trouble at school; he was hard to handle and Dad needed my support. Sometimes when I was at Dale Road I'd hear news about my sisters. From what Dad said I knew that Gin and Yasmin were talking to Lucy again. They weren't talking to me. Yasmin hasn't talked to me since the day I ran away. And when Ginda went back to Shinda she withdrew again.

It was Gin I saw first. I was out shopping on a Saturday morning a couple of weeks after we'd moved into Balfour Road and she was walking down the street towards me. The pavement was crowded but we were only about thirty metres apart and I'm sure she saw me. I raised my hand in greeting and a jolt of recognition jarred her face, but only for an instant. Then, with her head turned away, she crossed the road and I was left with my fingers stopped mid-flutter feeling stupid. I was gutted. It was fifteen years since I'd run away and still Gin could not forgive me.

I kept that sadness bottled up inside me. It was the start of my third year at university and I was trying to work out my schedule, making sure I gave enough time to Karma Nirvana and my studies. My main focus at college that year was a dissertation on Sikh women who had been disowned by their families. In the course of my reading I would discover that Guru Granth Sahib believed in equality between men and women and was against forced marriage as well as the caste system. Mum had always used his teachings as a weapon but I learnt they couldn't have been more different from what she taught me.

By the end of that term, I was pregnant again, fluttery with hope as I carried the life that was meant to put Raj and me back together again. We were so rarely together it's remarkable it happened, but I wasn't sorry. I thought it might help. How many women have made that mistake?

At three o'clock one February morning the phone rang. I was half awake anyway, my ears straining for the sound of Raj's key in the door. Maria was asleep beside me and Lisa was there, on a mattress on the floor; she was spending more and more time with me by then. I wanted to reach the phone before the ringing woke them up and I hurried downstairs, one hand instinctively covering my just swelling belly, goose-pimples rising in the pre-dawn chill.

'Hello?' As I grabbed the receiver I climbed onto the sofa, getting my feet off the cold, bare floor. 'Hello. Who's this?'

'I'm ringing to tell you that your husband is having an affair.'

It was a woman's voice, cool and silky and sounding rather pleased. I felt like I'd been punched in the stomach, '*What?*'

'Your husband is having an affair and I felt you ought to know.'

'I'm sorry, but who *are* you?'

'I thought you should know,' she said and then the line went dead.

I dropped the receiver and wrapped my arms around my belly. I remember rocking and howling like a madwoman as my fragile fantasy of happiness was shattered. Weeks of suspicion poured out of me as I gave myself over to sorrow.

I'd forgotten all about the kids until I heard a creak on the stairs. I looked up and saw Lisa, face frightened, shoulders hunched against the cold.

'What are you doing there? Get back to bed!' I bellowed at her, my poor vulnerable child. She fled and I went back to rocking, guilt now added to my misery. I was still huddled on the sofa, staring blankly at the grey dawn, when Raj came home at six o'clock.

He denied it. I probed and probed but he wouldn't admit to anything and in the end I gave up. I let life go on as it was because I couldn't see how to change it. I felt as powerless as I had in Nottingham. A few weeks later the woman rang again; she told me her name was Jane and said she knew me from my classes. That detail seemed so cruel.

By the time I was four months pregnant, my belly visibly swollen, my back beginning to ache, I was struggling to maintain the pretence that Raj and I could go on together. We shared nothing except a cold, crumbling house, Maria and the creation of the life that was growing inside me, a life that I was determined would grow up in an atmosphere of love. And where was love in the sour misery I carried with me through each day? In the sharp craving for affection? In the sullen moments of despair?

It was seeing my baby on the scan – thumb in his mouth,

ankles neatly crossed, heart pumping like a piston – that made my mind up.

The sonographer thought I was crying because she'd told me my baby was small for my dates and I didn't disillusion her. I accepted her comfort and kept my sorrow to myself. But as I lay there listening to her pointing out my baby's heart and lungs and liver ('all there, all healthy, your baby is going to be *fine*'), as I wiped the cold gel off my belly and struggled back into my clothes, as I made my next appointment and hurried back to the car, all that time something was hardening inside me. By the time I got home I'd made up my mind.

When Raj came in that afternoon I said, 'It's over, Raj, and I want you to go. Now. You know why. There's nothing to discuss. I'd like you to leave today.' Lisa was still at school and Maria at nursery; I'd planned it like that because I didn't want them to witness any ugly scene.

'Yeah, yeah.' He was standing there, nodding his head and grinning, like he'd heard it all before. I didn't argue or repeat myself. I picked up the phone and, with him there watching me, I phoned his dad.

'*Papa-ji*? I want you to know that it's over between me and Rajvinder because he's been having an affair. He's been seeing another woman for weeks and I can't pretend any more. I'm going to divorce him, *Papa-ji*, and I wanted you to know the reason why.'

I don't know if they believed me; I doubt Raj's mum did. But it mattered to me that I told them. I didn't want to take the blame. When I put the phone down Raj was still standing there, looking dumbfounded.

'I'm going now, to get the girls. I'll be out for a while. Please be gone when we get home.'

I never wavered. I'd thought I might go to pieces in the car, out of Raj's sight, but I didn't. I felt almost elated, stronger than I had in months. The next day I went out and bought a couple of tins of vivid pink paint and I covered the walls of the bedroom, working with a sort of manic energy. That was our main room, our only room really because it's where we kept our one electric heater. The girls played in there, I worked, we all slept there; after Raj left it was often the three of us in the double bed huddled together for warmth. I wanted to make it look bright to cheer us all up, to convince myself that the future was going to be all right and that night, with the still damp paint casting a rosy glow on the faces of my daughters as I kissed them, I thought it might be.

My confidence lasted about as long as it took to wash the smell of Raj from my sheets. A sense of failure dogged me. A few days after Raj had left, Lucy cut me dead in the street and I was actually glad; I couldn't face her. I was determined that Dad shouldn't find out what had happened and I'm pleased to say he never did.

I'd wake in the small hours, my chest tight, my heart fluttering, cold sweat on my back. Unable to sleep, I'd take my mind through the day ahead: the girls, Karma Nirvana, my dissertation, the baby growing inside me . . . I felt like a midget at the foot of a mountain. My sense of loneliness was over-whelming and, as it got light, it took all the willpower I had to drag myself out of bed.

At about seven o'clock I'd wake the girls and they'd sit on the bed eating cornflakes while I got ready. Cornflakes were cheap and there were bad weeks when they had them for every meal. I often went without; eating was too much effort. Lisa had chosen to live with me by then, but there were times when I sent her back to her dad because I was just too tired to keep pretending I was fine. I could feel her constantly watching me and the anxious look on her face wrung my heart. Maria was too little to notice. She'd go off for the day with Raj and come back babbling about the fun she'd had with him and Jane. The pain that caused me was as sharp as any knife.

With Raj gone we had no car, so each day I picked up a heavy bag of books and heaved Maria into my arms then ran to catch the bus. She would scream at me 'Stop jiggling me, Mummy, it hurts' and my heart would pump so fast I thought it might burst. I had to take Lisa first and then catch a different bus back to Maria's nursery before going on to Karma Nirvana.

Those days without a car almost broke me and my distress must have shown because it was during that week that my tutor first suggested I defer finishing my degree until the following year.

'I mean, look at yourself, Jasvinder, you're exhausted, anyone can see that. You're having a baby, you've got your job . . . does your husband help at all?'

'We're separated actually,' I said, biting down hard on my bottom lip to stop myself crying. I was okay until someone was kind to me.

'Well, all the more reason. Why drive yourself so hard? Lots of people defer. There's no shame in it – especially with such good reason.'

I smiled briefly. 'I don't want to. Thanks for your concern but I'll be fine.' I wouldn't even consider his suggestion. I was stressed, yes. But work was my only sanity.

My dissertation required a lot of research so I often went into university in the evenings. I'd get Maria from nursery and –

when she was with us – Lisa from her after-school club and we'd get there about six o'clock. First we'd go the refectory and get the girls some food. Things like beans and chips were cheap. Then I'd go to the library and look up the information I needed in journals and do some photocopying and collect any notes the tutors had left for me. At about eight I'd pick up the kids and take them home to bed.

I was in the habit of going in at weekends too by then. I'd take Lisa and Maria and ask the librarian if I could bring them in with me. I was completely honest with her, I just told her I really wanted to do this degree but I didn't have any childcare so I needed her help.

There was a corner of the library filled with children's books that were used by the students doing teacher training and she said Lisa and Maria could sit there as long as they were quiet. And they were quiet, bless them. Lisa was like a little mother to Maria, reading to her and playing with her for hours at a time. I never had to say a word. We'd have a break at lunchtime. I can remember sitting on the same bench in the freezing grey days of February and the hot sun of May. We'd eat the sandwiches I'd brought and then go for a little walk in the grounds before going back to the library. I did that every Saturday and Sunday for about two years.

My days were so full I had no time to think but come the evening, with the girls settled, my thoughts began to spiral. Loneliness grew inside me. I'd failed at every relationship I'd tried to make and I hated myself for it. By day I fought for the rights of Asian women and by night I craved acceptance from the very community I'd rejected. I sat huddled in a blanket with my sociology books open, staring at the same page for what felt like hours on end, willing the information to sink in. I longed for company. I'd set myself up as a pioneer but what I wanted to be was ordinary. I wanted a family.

It must have been spring when Raj and I finally separated but when I look back I remember all the days as dark and grey. I see myself as cold and hunched, pulled in, as if nursing a physical injury. I thought a lot about death. Oblivion seemed so alluring. I had all these suicide plans and I think if the baby hadn't started kicking I'd have done it. It was the baby that stopped me, the baby, Maria and Lisa.

29

One day, when I was really low, I rang Karma Nirvana and asked for a few days off. The chairwoman told me to take as long as I needed. 'You should have some maternity leave anyway, Jas,' she said. And I was grateful. The state I was in I wasn't fit for support work; I barely had anything inside myself to give my kids, let alone anyone else.

I might have collapsed completely had it not been for Trish, who heard what had happened from my chairwoman. Our paths must have been criss-crossing since the day I made the presentation at the women's centre, but somehow we rarely met. She turned up on my doorstep one evening at about nine o'clock, after the girls were in bed.

'Hello, Jasvinder,' she said. 'Don't think me nosy, but I've come to see if you need help with anything. I heard your husband left you. Can I come in?'

She walked into my life and made it her business to look after me. In the bleak weeks that followed Trish became my saviour. She brought round nourishing food and forced me into eating properly, she listened to my woes and made me laugh. When I was at my lowest ebb she took me to live with her for a fortnight, even giving up her bed for me and Maria and sleeping on the sofa. She became my friend, the best friend I've ever had.

When necessary, Trish minded the girls for me as I attended what felt like endless hospital appointments. I'd had completely straightforward pregnancies with Lisa and – until my placenta abrupted – with Maria too, but this one was full of problems. The baby was small and I was so strung up that I kept fainting and having palpitations. I was closely monitored.

By May the baby was kicking hard; heels, knees and elbows jabbed my belly. As he became more and more real to me I dreaded bringing him back to the drab dereliction of Balfour Road where, by that stage, you could almost taste the sadness in the air. I made enquiries and found that with my Karma Nirvana salary I could get a tiny mortgage. I told Trish and she encouraged me. A desire to move was added to my stress.

At my six-month appointment my blood pressure was so high the doctor wanted to admit me to hospital for monitoring.

'But I can't come in. I'm a single mother, I've got kids to look after. And I'm taking my finals in a month, I've got a dissertation to finish. I've got so much work to do, honestly I can't come into hospital.'

The doctor said I had to, for the sake of the baby. He sent me up to the ward straight away and Trish, bless her, sorted everything out. The girls went to their dads' and after work that day Trish brought me in washing things and something to sleep in and a pile of books. Those were the only things I really wanted. I lay in bed, wired up to a monitor, working through my files. Trish had told my tutor and he was really supportive; he even arranged to have some lecture notes sent in to me.

I did rest though. Once I was lying down tiredness hit me like a truck. For the first time in months I slept through the night and two or three times a day I'd find myself nodding off, book in hand. I'd been there about four days when I woke from a nap to see Jassey sitting beside me. I was astonished. After he'd got residence rights for Lisa and I'd married Raj there had been nothing but bitterness between us. I hadn't seen him for about four years. I remember thinking that he looked older, that he'd put on weight.

'Is Lisa okay?' I asked, instantly anxious.

'Yeah, yeah, she's fine. It's not her I've come about.' He paused, looking uncomfortable, but then carried right on.

'Look, Jas, I wanted to say I'm sorry it didn't work out for you and Raj. I've heard it's been really hard for you. Lisa's told me a bit, and other people, you know what the grapevine is like.' He gave a wry smile. 'I wanted to say I'm sorry, and also that I'd like you to come back to me, Jas, I mean it. I'd accept your children as my own, Maria and this one.' He made a little bow towards the bump beneath the sheet. 'I'd marry you again and we'd be a family, I'd look after you . . .' He paused, his cheeks flushed, and fixed me with the open, completely honest gaze I remembered so clearly. 'I mean it, Jas, what do you think?'

For an instant a picture of his house – our house – flashed through my mind: the pink-painted living-room, the flower-filled garden, tomatoes in my greenhouse. I thought about sharing responsibilities and not worrying about money every second of every day. I looked into Jassey's kind, hopeful eyes and thought about companionship. It could all be so easy.

'No, Jassey,' I said. 'I'm grateful for the offer, really. But it wouldn't work, you know that. You don't deserve to be hurt all over again.'

30

The day my finals started was very hot. By 10 a.m. my clothes were sticking to me. I was seven months pregnant and my bump ached. I remember the sense of tension as we all stood outside the exam room fanning ourselves with our hands. When the doors of the examination hall were opened all you could see was an army of desks set out with rigid precision. Even the exam papers seemed to have been laid down perfectly straight. We'd all been given desk numbers; I found mine and sat down, glad to do so because my head was swimming. The windows, high up in the walls, were open but the room was close.

The first hour passed quickly. The air was thick and still with concentration. I felt lucky with the questions and had no trouble recalling the facts I needed, my pen seemed to skim across the page. But halfway through the second essay my energy began to flag. Pinpricks of light danced before my eyes. I felt light-headed and wished I'd had some breakfast. As I put up my hand to ask for a glass of water the dancing pinpricks became a wall of white light that blinded me. My desk seemed to tilt and the floor was rising up . . .

I dimly remember hands lifting me, my feet clumsy on the floor, a cool room with a fan, a slim hand holding out a glass of water. I heard a voice telling me to relax, there was no more to worry about. 'But I didn't finish the paper. I've got to go back. The exam isn't over.' I tried to get up but the nurse put a restraining hand on my shoulder.

'It's over for you, dear. You can't go back in once you've left the exam hall.'

'But I have to. I've *got* to finish.' Suddenly I recognized the woman standing behind the nurse as one of the invigilators; it was Professor Sharma, who I knew and liked. 'Did you bring me here?' She nodded. 'Well, then you know exactly what happened. You know I haven't cheated. You have to let me go back in. Please, this means so much to me. And I feel fine now, honestly.'

The nurse and the invigilator exchanged glances. I could see them weighing rules against reason and whether or not I was fit enough to finish the paper. Ungainly and feeling heavy as a heifer I swung my legs off the couch and stood up, determined to convince them I was fine.

'All right then, you win. But let's be quick.' The invigilator led the way back to the exam hall and as we reached its doors, looked at her watch. 'It's twelve-fifteen. You came out at five to twelve. I'll arrange for you to have an extra twenty minutes at the end, so don't put your pen down when the others do.'

I got through the exams. I finally handed in my dissertation. Three years of study ended but I didn't feel jubilant. At the end of my last exam I left the hall caught up in a stream of excited students. I pushed my way to the side and stood back against the wall to let them pass, feeling old and tired as I watched them laughing, high five-ing one another, screwing up their notes as they danced their way across the campus to celebrate in the pub. I wouldn't have joined them, even if they'd asked me to. Completing the degree meant nothing to me; I'd always known I had the willpower to complete it. What mattered to me was passing it and I wasn't going to celebrate until I knew I'd done that. I hurried to the car park, keen to be on time to pick up Maria and Lisa.

The baby was due in August and with every week that passed I became more determined to move out of Balfour Road: the thought of four of us living in its one habitable room was terrible. But I wasn't prepared to walk away with nothing as I had done when I left Jassey. As I saw it, Raj was the guilty party and if he wanted me out of the house, he'd have to buy me out of it.

I wanted to move out of the Asian area. It made me feel claustrophobic, just as I'd felt in White's View. I'd grown used to my sisters snubbing me but I resented the way disapproval spread through the community. Try as I might I couldn't ignore the curious stares, the reproving glances, the way women drew aside in huddles keeping their children close when I went in and out of shops around Balfour Road. I knew I was gossip-fodder and I hated it.

I'd found a house about four miles away in Oakwood. It was tiny, but it was detached and it had three bedrooms. I went to see it with Trish and the girls one July afternoon and all the rooms were really sunny. I remember Maria lying on the carpet in a beam of light and saying, 'Look, Mummy, I'm sunbathing indoors.' All the rooms had carpet; we kicked off our sandals and walked about barefoot just for the pleasure of the soft, clean feel of it. Everything was so finished compared with Balfour Road; to Lisa's delight there was even a Jacuzzi in the bathtub. And it had a garden, just a scrubby little lawn with a couple of neglected flower beds, but I could imagine the baby there, sleeping in the sunshine in his pram.

I made an offer straight away and stayed up late that night, juggling figures, working out how I could possibly afford it. I was getting cleverer with money by then. In my three-year struggle through university I'd got used to searching for loans, grants, hardship funds – anything that would allow me to complete my studies. I'd learnt by then that there was help available, but only if you asked for it.

I went into labour on 12 August 1997. I was woken by the first, unmistakeable cramps, and I remember thinking 'I'm so tired, I don't know if I can do this'. I got myself to the hospital and Trish joined me there. Raj had asked her to, because he was working. Trish was wonderful; she stayed with me as I laboured, rubbing my back, smoothing my hair off my face, holding my hand when the midwife examined me. With every contraction I felt like I was being flattened.

Raj arrived just as I was being prepared for a Caesarean, all ready to prove himself the attentive, anxious father. I'd wanted a normal delivery, but the midwives had convinced me that wasn't going to happen. I was really scared and I wanted Trish right beside me, but when Raj arrived it was all 'Ah, here's the father', and calling him in and squeezing Trish out and I was so out of it I couldn't do anything. But when the midwives said, 'It's a boy, Jasvinder', when they gave him to me, wrapped in a little blue blanket, Trish's squeals of joy were the loudest. I'll never forget those cries of jubilation. I looked down at him, fanned out his tiny fist, checked he was perfect and then, as they finished stitching me, I thought, 'It's over, please someone take this baby and let me get some sleep'.

The children and I moved in to Calver Close, Oakwood when Joshua was two weeks old. It wasn't much of a move; just clothes and books and the tatty old mattress from Balfour Road. I didn't want to take anything from there, but Raj said I should take it and we didn't have any other sort of bed so I swallowed my pride in order to be practical.

I remember our first night in that house. We all slept in one room, me, Lisa and Maria on the mattress and Joshua on the floor beside us in his little Moses basket. There were no curtains and moonlight streamed through the window and lit up the faces of my sleeping children. Lisa with her long black hair strewn across the pillow and her brow slightly furrowed, anxious even in her sleep; Maria, thumb in her mouth, pressed tight in beside me and Joshua, flat on his back with his arms thrown back beside his head, his tiny chest rising and falling beneath his pale blue sleepsuit. His mouth was making little sucking movements and I knew he'd wake soon for a feed because my breasts felt hot and swollen.

I propped myself up on my elbows and lay there waiting for his cry, ready to scoop him up and hold him close before his hungry wails woke Maria and Lisa. I was tired but that night I also felt exhilarated. I took a deep, satisfied breath and caught the scent from Trish's roses. She'd brought them round earlier, all ready in a vase, and they were sitting on the windowsill, a bright splash of promise. I was proud of myself and I don't know that I'd ever before felt that. I'd bought a house, a house that was mine alone, and I was going to make it a home for my children. I might be exiled from my family and its history, but I suddenly felt confident that we could make it on our own.

Next morning, while I was feeding Joshua, Lisa rummaged in my old box of books and found herself a pen and paper and we started making a list of goals: things that we were going to save for.

'I'm going to have a bed for myself,' she said.

'I'm going to have a bed for myself and a television,' I countered.

'I'm going to have a bed for myself, and a television and something to put my clothes in.'

'I'm going to have a bed for myself and a television and a car that I can rely on to get us down the motorway . . .'

That was nine years ago and it was the start of a game that's never ended. 'Speak what you want, Lisa, even if it seems a million miles away,' that's what I told her. 'Speak what you want because once you've sown that seed you can work towards it.'

My results from Derby University arrived a few days after we'd moved in. I picked the envelope off the mat and stood there staring at it. Inside was the piece of paper that would realize or dissolve the dream I'd worked so hard for. It was five minutes before I could bring myself to open it. Then, as I pulled the flimsy paper out of the envelope and unfolded it my hands were shaking so much that I could hardly focus on the word First.

'First! Lisa, Maria, Lisa, I got a First. Quick, come and look. I got a First.' The girls came running and we were shouting, laughing, dancing up and down the tiny passage until Joshua took fright at all the noise and started howling. I took him from his basket, kissed him, soothed him, sat down on the mattress to feed him. The girls flopped down beside me and Maria, leaning against me, said, 'Mummy, what's a First?'

I freeze-framed those minutes with the four of us sitting on the mattress. I did it deliberately and even today I can play them through my mind like a video: five minutes of hard-earned, perfect happiness.

When my tutor, Graham Fowler, rang a few weeks later I thought he was going to congratulate me, and he did. But then he asked if I would give the vote of thanks on behalf of the students on graduation day. I was overwhelmed by the honour, it was the last thing I'd expected. With 3,000 students in the university, why pick me? He said it was because I'd worked so hard and overcome so much to finish my degree, which surprised me because I'd tried to hide my situation from my tutors. I hadn't wanted them feeling sorry for me; my training in secrecy was dying hard.

When the day came I felt sick with excitement and nerves. I'd hired a mortar board and gown and I wore them over a dark suit and a scarlet shirt; I wanted to look smart. The main hall was packed with chairs. We graduates were all sitting in the front rows and our guests were behind us. I remember craning round, scanning each row of people. I spotted Raj. Jane had walked out on him by then and he was single again. I'd said he could come because I needed someone to hold Joshua. He was sitting between Maria and Lisa with Joshua on his lap and I found myself looking at him quite dispassionately. I knew I'd shut that door for ever and I was never going back. It was my dad I was really looking for. I'd invited him but he'd been noncommittal. I so wanted him there.

I hadn't found him by the time the Chancellor of the University started speaking. He introduced the guests – Dame Helena Kennedy was there to collect an honorary degree, she's the only one I remember – before addressing us all. Then in a long slow crocodile every single graduate filed up onto the stage to be presented with their certificate. The Chancellor shook each hand and had a quick word with everyone; it seemed to take for ever. And then it was me.

My legs felt like jelly and my hands were clammy as I stood behind the lectern. I was still looking for Dad as the Chancellor introduced me. I'd have given anything to have seen him sitting there, staring up at me. I wanted to see his face, pleased and proud as he watched his only graduate daughter in her mortar board and gown. The applause following the Chancellor's words was brief, and then there was this enormous silence, which I had to fill.

Graham had said to speak for fifteen minutes and in the end I think I managed ten. I was shaking when I started. I hadn't made any notes but somehow I knew what I was going to say. It wasn't anything grand.

I started by telling them about the day I first set foot on the campus, more than five years previously, when I was looking for a place to do my A levels. I told them how *mortified* I was to find out it was a university because that seemed so high above my station. I told them how I ran off with my tail between my legs, and that made them laugh.

The laughter relaxed me. I found myself saying what it was like doing A levels at the age of twenty-seven, having scarcely opened a book since I'd left school. I explained that my reasons for doing those exams were practical – I wanted to be able to support myself – but that once I'd started, the books had brought me so much unexpected pleasure. Reading had opened up a whole new world for me.

I said I'd been teased for being a mature student, and I explained what it had felt like being a single mother, pregnant and doing a degree. I said how very, very hard it had been and how my tutors had done everything they could to help me, right down to suggesting that I defer my degree. 'I could never have done that,' I said. 'I wanted this degree so badly, it meant so much to me, that from somewhere – and even today I don't know where – I got the determination to keep going, to see it right through to the final exam. And I'm so glad I did because when I opened that envelope saying I'd passed, that I'd got a higher grade than I ever expected, I nearly burst with pride at my achievement. Seeing that word First was one of the best moments of my life. But that is just the start for me, I'm sure of that.'

I had to pause for breath then and there was a spatter of applause across the audience, but I suddenly realized that I hadn't finished, that I had something else to say, so I raised my hand up off the lectern to make them stop.

'My mum and dad came here in the 1950s to look for work,' I said, and I could feel the audience settle down as they sensed something different coming. 'They came here from the Punjab, to a country they didn't know, with a language they didn't speak, far, far from everything familiar to them, so that they could give me, my brother and my sisters, a better chance in life. It's taken me a long time to realize how much they gave up for us, how much they sacrificed to make sure that we had the opportunities they never had. I may not always have seen eye to eye with my parents, I may not have shared their values, but I'm grateful, so grateful to them for that.'

There was another bit of clapping but I didn't stop for it, I went right on. 'I'm pleased to say I seized those opportunities, I can look back now and say I grabbed them and made the most of them and that's why I'm standing here today. If someone like me, who left school with no qualifications, who came to university a single mum with two kids, and had another on the way, if someone like me can get qualifications, anyone can. And I look forward to seeing my kids following in my footsteps. I want to see you on this stage one day, Lisa, and you, Maria, and Joshua.'

I stopped then and the whole place exploded with clapping. Everyone stood up. Dame Helena Kennedy came over and kissed me, and she had tears pouring down her face. It was extraordinary. The applause seemed to go on and on, and while I was stood there, waiting for it finish, I was still looking for my dad. Finally, just before I left the stage, I faced the fact he wasn't there. I didn't blame him. Some of my family wouldn't have liked him coming. I understood that, but it didn't make the hurt I felt any easier to bear.

I went round to see him a few days later. I took him a framed copy of my graduation photograph and told him that the speech went well. He didn't say much but he did look pleased and to me that meant a lot.

31

With my degree over and Joshua settled into a routine, I went back to Karma Nirvana with a burst of new energy. Towards the end of my first week back a ward sister at the local hospital rang to see if we could send someone to talk to a young Asian girl brought in by a stranger who had found her collapsed in the street. Her name was Zainab.

I took the call and felt concerned immediately. Sister said the doctors thought she'd swallowed something highly toxic; judging by the marks and the smell on her clothes it was probably bleach. Although she had been admitted almost a week before no one had been in to visit her, no one had even rung to enquire. The stranger who picked her up couldn't tell them anything except the area of Derby in which he found her and she didn't seem to have been carrying a bag or anything else that might tell them who she was.

'All we've got out of her is her name. But it's clear she doesn't speak English. Would anyone from your team have time . . . ?'

'Of course, I'll come myself, I'll come tomorrow,' I said, running my next day's appointments through my mind as I spoke. I knew it would be a squeeze, but support work is the basis of everything Karma Nirvana does and to this day I make it a priority. I went in first thing next morning and a nurse directed me towards a bed occupied by someone so tiny that she hardly made a bump beneath the sheets. All I could see was a mess of dark hair on the pillow and a tangle of tubes leading up to various drips. I walked across and stood beside the bed.

She turned her head towards me; her face was yellowish grey. For a second I thought I saw a spark of curiosity in her huge, dark eyes, but then she sighed, as if the whole thing was too much effort, and looked away.

'I've come to see you, to help you if I can.' I drew a chair up to the bed. I didn't say anything else. Fear pulsated off her almost palpably and instinct told me to go very slowly. I put my hand over hers where it was lying limply on the bedspread and sat quietly for about half an hour. Then I got up. 'I've got to go now, but I'll come back tomorrow.'

She turned her head again and this time held my gaze.

Over the next few days I visited that girl as often as I could. She was one of those people – there have been a few since Karma Nirvana started – who got under my skin. Supporting them has become an important part of my life. When we first met there was something about her complete desolation that I recognized from my own dark days in Newcastle.

Sitting beside her, I told her about that time in my life, I told her the whole story right down to my still being estranged from my family. It had helped me get through to Ayesha and I hoped it might have the same effect now. She listened to me silent and wide-eyed and when I got to the bit about having to finally accept that my mum cared more about the community than she did about me, tears began to pour down her face. I stopped talking and she cried for about five minutes before she dried her eyes and said, in Punjabi, 'I know how that feels.'

It had taken until she was strong enough to sit in the chair beside her bed for a couple of hours each day for me to be able to coax a few words out of her, and the sister had been right, she spoke no English. The way her eyes would go glassy with fear and confusion as they fixed on the face of the person speaking reminded me so much of Mum. The doctors wanted to know exactly what she'd swallowed and although she didn't want to talk about it – I think she was ashamed of what she'd done – she eventually admitted it was household bleach. Half a bottle of it. 'You can tell her she's lucky she's not dead,' said the doctor who'd asked me to find out. 'She may well find that her digestion has been permanently damaged.'

She crept down the road to recovery. One mild October day I asked the ward sister if I could take her for a walk in the hospital grounds. We went very slowly; it took quite a time to work our way through the maze of corridors and Zainab was already tired by the time we made it outside into the fresh air. There was a bench a few hundred yards from the exit doors and we decided to stroll over and rest on that. Zainab sat there with her eyes closed and her face tilted up towards the sky taking in great gulps of air. She looked like someone really thirsty who'd been given a drink.

The ward sister had told me as I left the day before that I was still Zainab's only visitor. 'She's got her social worker now, and she's trying to decide what's to be done with her when she's ready to leave. We still don't know anything about her. Will you find out what you can?' I said I would. I felt Zainab trusted me by then.

I began very gently; I asked her if, when she left hospital, she'd be going back to her family. Her eyes widened in alarm and she shook her head vigorously.

'Where is your family, Zainab? Sister says she hasn't heard from them since you came into hospital. Do they know you're here?'

She shrugged and a shadow of the desolation I first knew in her flashed across her face. 'My mother and father are in Pakistan. I don't know if they know I'm here. My husband – he's my father's cousin – is here in Derby. He's probably told them that I've run away.' She dropped her head and the bitterness in her voice was blunted by tears. 'My father will be so angry with me; I've shamed him, but I couldn't stay there any longer, they were so cruel,' she sobbed.

I held her hand as she told me how her husband had raped her the week she arrived in England. 'I didn't know him. We didn't meet until the wedding; I was sixteen and I was shy. For three days he was patient but then he forced me . . .' Her cheeks flushed with shame, but having started her story, the indignities she had suffered poured out. 'He hurt me so badly I didn't want to do it again, so he kept on raping me. He hurt me so much, but I had no time to rest. Every morning I had to get up at six and do housework, make the meals, wash the clothes, clean the rooms. They treated me like a servant. Sometimes I did not sit down until ten at night, and if I was slow or missed something, my mother-in-law would beat me. When I wasn't working, she would lock me in my room. For two years I didn't walk outside in the streets, Jasvinder.' Her voice was flat and sad.

'Why didn't you tell someone? You should have told the police,' I said. I had my arm tight round Zainab's shoulders now. It was as if I was trying to press feeling into her, all the love and care she'd been starved of for years. For all the trust between us, she still felt tense and rigid in my grip.

'How could I? I don't . . .'

'. . . speak English.' I finished the sentence for her. 'Of course, how stupid of me.'

'And it's not just that. I was never alone; even at the doctor's my husband or my mother-in-law would come in to the appointment with me. And anyway, my mother-in-law said if the police or anybody else in authority knew I was here I'd be arrested and put in prison for being here illegally. That's what she said. Is it true, Jasvinder?'

I reassured her that it wasn't and led her gently back inside again. She was obviously exhausted. I was tired too, but once I'd said goodbye to her I went to the Karma Nirvana offices and rang the number Sister had given me for Zainab's social worker. I told her all I'd learnt and she promised to try to find safe accommodation for Zainab when she was ready to leave hospital. 'I think she'll need someone to keep an eye on her,' I said. I wasn't sure Zainab shared her doctor's opinion that she was lucky to be alive.

When I'd put the phone down I sat there for a few minutes, preoccupied, haunted by the last thing Zainab had said to me, her eyes dark with pain. 'The social worker wants to contact my parents; she doesn't understand how angry they would be. I am their daughter, but if they knew what I'd done they would disown me. My parents care more about honour than they do about me.'

I know what that feels like. I've been there. I understood her anguished disbelief. How could anyone turn their back on their own child for the sake of a concept? How could that be considered honourable? To me it seemed a cause of shame.

*   *   *

Zainab was released from hospital into a Derby refuge and I went to see her there a couple of days after she'd arrived. It was a nice enough place, shabby but well looked after. The staff were friendly and keen to help, but there were no Punjabi speakers among them so Zainab was reliant on an interpreter who only came sporadically.

I'd found her sitting on her bed which, according to the refuge staff, was where she spent all her time. She looked totally dejected and withdrawn. The room was small: just big enough for a single bed, a narrow hanging cupboard and a small chest of drawers. In an effort to brighten the place up someone had stuck a travel poster to the wall, advertising holidays in France. Save for her actual presence there was nothing to show it was Zainab's room. She'd left her in-laws' house with nothing; she had nothing.

It suddenly occurred to me that, although she must have been in Britain for two years, incarceration in her in-laws' house meant Zainab knew almost nothing of this country or its people. Her suicide attempt had caused her to be picked up and dumped, unprepared and empty-handed, into a western way of life. She had nothing familiar to cling to.

'How do you get on with the other people here?' I asked her. She shrugged. 'They only speak English. They can't talk to me, so they ignore me, and they go like this —' she wrinkled her nose in a show of disgust and waved her hand in front of her face — 'when I make Indian tea . . . It is better that I stay here by myself.'

I'd heard similar comments made by some of the women who visited our surgeries. 'In the end I couldn't stand the loneliness so I went back home.' 'They kept suggesting I call my mother and tell her where I was.' 'The other women kept their kids away from mine . . .' But it was the first time I'd seen it for myself. It dawned on me that there might be a case for specialist provision for Asian women and as I sat beside Zainab on her bed that afternoon I made two resolutions. The first was to get Zainab to sign herself up for English lessons. The second was to find myself some shift work in the local refuges; I needed to know more.

32

In August 1999 a man called Mohinder rang me out of the blue. I'd known him when I was a child because he spent a lot of time with Prakash. She helped his family settle in Britain and I'd been brought up to call him *Py-ji* which means brother. I knew he'd got married, had two kids and moved to Derby but I hadn't seen him for years.

'I need to talk to you, Jas. Can you come round to my place?'

I was suspicious. 'What is it? Can't we just talk on the phone?'

'No, no, we need to see each other face to face. But you won't regret it, believe me. Why not come round tomorrow afternoon. Say five o'clock?'

I agreed. I was still uneasy but I was curious. Next day I knocked on his door at precisely five o'clock. It was a big house, right in the Asian area; he'd obviously done well for himself.

'Ah, Jas, come in, come in. How about some tea?' he said, leading me through to the kitchen. He was making out that he was all hospitable but I could tell he was nervous: his face was covered with a light film of sweat.

'No thanks, *Py-ji*. Why don't you just tell me what you want to talk about?'

'Ah yes. Well, the thing is this, Jasvinder, I have managed to find you a suitable match.'

'You've done *what*?'

'I've found a husband for you. Be realistic, Jas. Who is going to want you now? Three children and two divorces to your name – who will look at you? Your family was good to me and now, in return, I have made it my business to help you. He is a good man, believe me. He is an accountant, good job. And he is currently in Leeds. I will arrange everything, don't worry. Just say the word and I will get the papers so you can sponsor him into the country . . .'

I was dumbfounded, so surprised – and angry – that I couldn't say anything. I just stood there looking at him. He would have run on and on if my mobile phone hadn't interrupted him.

It was Sunny and his husky fifteen-year-old's mumble had been replaced by a clear voice, tight with panic.

'*Massi-ji*? You've got to come quick. It's Dad. I think he's dead.'

I didn't need telling twice. It was the way Sunny said 'think' that made me shut off all emotion and move as quickly as I could. If I got there fast it might not be too late. I was half way to the front door when I shouted over my shoulder, 'I'm going to my dad's. Call an ambulance. Sunny thinks he's dead.'

It took me less than ten minutes to get to Dale Road. The front door was on the latch and I ran right through it to where Dad was lying on the living-room floor. His mouth was open and his skin was grey. Sunny was crouched down beside him, tears streaming down his face.

I was down on my knees and trying to remember years back

when St John's Ambulance came to Littleover School and showed us mouth-to-mouth resuscitation. I pinched Dad's nose and, covering his mouth with mine, tried to breathe life back into him. His skin was cold but not icy and I thought that must be good. I breathed into him once, twice, three times and each time I turned my head to fill my own lungs I saw his chest rise and fall. I breathed into him a fourth time and as his chest fell with the exhalation it gave a sort of rattle. I thought he coughed.

'I think he's coming back, Sunny,' I said, and redoubled my efforts. I was pressing on his chest now too, taking it in turns to breathe and press, breathe and press. I was frantic, trying to pump life back into him. I was still doing it when the ambulance men came and told me, very gently, that he was dead.

They took him to the hospital and I followed in my car with Sunny and Mohinder, who'd followed me to the house. My sisters were there, screaming and crying.

Sunny was beside himself that evening as we waited in the hospital. He'd been playing football with his mates when Dad had his heart attack and he kept saying if only he'd been home he might have saved him. I tried to console him and the others did too. Concern for him was the only thing that linked us; other than that there was nothing between us but awkward space.

Later, when the doctor said we could go, I went back to lock Dad's house up. I'd thought I'd spend some time there but I couldn't, I couldn't even bring myself to go upstairs. The house was already full of ghosts. In the living-room I looked down at the spot where I'd tried to bring Dad back and thought about my mouth against his and how I'd tried to force life back into him. For most of my life Dad had kept me at arm's length and then, at the point of his death, I'd been so close to him it was obscene.

Back in Oakwood I hugged my kids a little tighter, held them a little longer than I normally would. Joshua was only two but he sat on my knee and wiped the tears off my cheeks with his sticky little hands: 'I love your dad, Mummy,' he said. Lisa was really cut up. She'd become quite close to Dad.

They moved him from the hospital morgue to the chapel of rest and I went to see him there. I'd been told I could spend as long as I liked with him and I stayed quite a while. I wanted him to have company; I hated the fact that he'd died all alone. On the living-room floor he'd been dishevelled, with his wispy hair spread out everywhere, but now someone had made him look all neat and tidy. He seemed at peace and talking to him seemed so natural. I had all the time I needed because, after all those years, he didn't have to worry about other people knowing I was with him.

I talked to him about the time we used to spend together on the allotments and how much that had meant to me. I reminded him of the old car he used to drive us to school in; how its wipers didn't work and how he used to make me lean out of the window and wipe the snow off as he drove along. I told him how much I loved him and how I wished things had been different between us. I said I knew how hard his life had been here in England and how brave I thought he and Mum had been to leave India, to make that sacrifice for us. I wondered – I still do – what my life would have been like if he had stayed on his farm in the Punjab. The last thing I said was that I would look after Sunny for him, always.

I was very grateful to be able to stand by my dad's body and say all that. I felt I said things I'd been keeping bottled up for years. I couldn't do it when Mum died because my sisters wouldn't let me near her; they washed the body and did all those things for her. I asked if I could help but they wouldn't let me: 'If the hands of an outcast touch her she'll be contaminated,' that's what they said.

This time I'd hardly got home from the chapel of rest when Gin rang. 'We've got to get this funeral organized,' she said, as if we went through a 'to do list' together every day. 'You have to get him a suit; you'll have to put a suit on him.'

After the mouth-to-mouth, that was the second most personal thing I ever did for my dad. I didn't know what size he was so I drove round to his house and measured his best suit, his only suit, the one that smelt like him, hair oil and cigarettes. Then I went into town and went round the shops trying to find the suit he'd want to wear for all eternity. He'd turned away from me in life but I was looking after him in death. I was talking to him in my head, telling him how strange that felt.

Sunny wanted to buy him some dark socks with cartoon characters on them so I got those and then, from the house, we fetched a couple of things to put in the coffin. The only one I remember is a picture of Mum. We dressed him up in the suit and the socks and the new brown tie I'd bought him and he looked so smart. I think Mum would have been proud.

After the funeral, when I was ready, I went back to Dale Road to start packing up Dad's things. I was the one my family had never wanted in the house, the one who was always having to scuttle off and make herself scarce, but now Mum and Dad were gone there I was, all by myself, clearing up. I just got on with it.

In the fridge I found the last lot of fruit I'd brought him. It was hard to make him eat properly after Mum died. I tried buying vitamins, but he said he couldn't remember to take them. He was tired and diminished. Even though Sunny was living there with him he seemed so alone.

I was upstairs, doing his bedroom, when I saw my graduation picture on the wall. I hadn't seen it since the day I gave it to him and I thought he'd put it away and forgotten about it, but there it was. It was in the corner, not in a prominent place, but it was on the wall all right. Dad couldn't say how proud he was of me in life, but I suddenly felt he was saying it in death. I took the photograph down and I'm looking at it now.

We had to go to the solicitors to have the will read. I'd driven Dad there to have it drawn up but I had no idea what it contained because I'd sat outside until he was ready for me to drive him home again. The first thing the solicitor said was that Dad had made me and Ginda executors of his will. To me that spoke volumes. I had never expected to be the one holding the keys to his property and dealing with his matters. I always thought it would be Balbir because he was the only son and sons are so precious in Asian families. Besides, I was the one who dishonoured the family.

That's what they all said for years, but in the end it turned out differently. Dad spoke to me in death. At the end, it was me he trusted to do the right thing. I still miss him. I still wish I'd told him I loved him before it was too late, told him and my mum. But I'm glad of the things he said to me when he died and I've tried my best to carry out his wishes, even though it's sometimes been hard.

Dad left everything to Sunny. Ginda walked out of the solicitor's office in disgust when she heard that. To me it seemed fair: Sunny had no one else in the world and anyway, who were we to question what Dad wanted?

33

The summer after Dad died, Lucy arrived on my doorstep unannounced. I was her last resort. Lucy had wanted to stay with Gin, but Gin's husband hadn't forgiven her. The truce between them was always uneasy. She had abandoned her arranged marriage with his nephew – to him that was hugely shameful.

Of course I said she could stay. I still had dreams of us being a proper family then. That summer Lucy seemed sad. One night she and I started to talk about our upbringing and why our mother was the way she was. I told Lucy:

'I think she and Dad both thought they were doing the best for us.' I was telling her what I'd so often told myself. I'd worked hard to accept that as the truth. I wanted to put my childhood to rest and leave my bitterness behind.

'But she never showed love for us, she never hugged us or kissed us . . .' Lucy was beside herself, but what could I say?

The love Mum showed was conditional. It was dependent on us being what she hoped for and expected: diligent daughters, obedient wives, dutiful daughters-in-law, model Asian citizens. I believe now that those were the things she thought would make us happy, keep us safe.

When I was young I thought my mum was motivated by arrogance. Her obsession with the hierarchy of caste, with the family's reputation, with our honour, I thought all those things were signs of her pride. Now I wonder if she was driven by fear. In some ways she and Dad were just like I was when I ran away: displaced persons, severed from their roots and families. In England their precious community was the only framework they could cling to, the only familiar thing they had.

I've come to terms with my childhood. I feel close to Mum and Dad, even though they are dead. As for my siblings, they're not family in any real sense. We don't talk to each other now.

Most of the news about my family I get second-hand. I read in the local paper that Balbir set fire to a carpet in his house. It was attempted suicide but, because of the risk to his neighbours, he was done for arson and ended up in prison. Sunny told me Balbir was beaten up while he was there for being the brother of 'that bitch who helps girls run away from home'.

Sunny was my link with the family but in the past few months that's changed. Inasmuch as I could I treated him as my own. The year after Dad died I sold my house in Oakwood and moved back into the Asian area. I bought a place on Warwick Avenue, just as I said I would when we were on the school run, all those years ago. I did it for Sunny so that he could come and live with us without moving away from everything he knew.

In 2002, when Sunny was eighteen, I kept my promise to Robina and took him to Canada to meet his dad, Navtej. On that first visit we were welcomed and fêted and treated like kings. Navtej had remarried but he never had another child. He said he'd like Sunny to come and live with him and, a year later, Sunny went.

I can't say I was sorry. Since he'd reached his teens Sunny had been questioning my values: 'Why do you do the work you do?' 'Why can't you be like Ginda-*masi*?' 'How can you let Lisa have a boyfriend?'

Sunny went to live in Canada but he wasn't happy.

He rang night after night after night, until I agreed to fly over and sort things out. This time there was no welcome. A family meeting to discuss Sunny's future became a furious row. All the old insults were hurled at me: 'You married a *chamar*, you disgraced your family, you're no better than a prostitute . . .' We packed our bags and left and there's been no contact since.

My story became Sunny's story. His family was no more able to accept Sunny's individuality than my parents could accept mine. In the Asian community the will of the family still comes first.

I tried to help him with his life. I always knew he was ashamed of what I do, but when I heard he was saying to people, 'When I marry I won't let my wife talk to my *masi*', I challenged him. We're not talking any more, which makes me very sad.

I've moved away from him, I've moved away from all of them. I got used to living in the Asian area because I'm strong enough now not to care what people think. But the day Gin and Yasmin ignored Lisa and Maria out in the street – deliberately cut them dead – I decided I was moving. I'm not exposing my kids to the hurt I've known; I'm not handing down that legacy of rejection.

Three years ago I bought a house in a little place just outside Derby. I joke that I'm the only Asian in the village but the fact is, I love that. I'm away from my work, away from the community into which I've never fitted comfortably. I can come home and shut the door and nobody bothers me; I am at peace.

Lisa has left home now. Last year, aged twenty-one, she graduated in law from Leeds University and I nearly burst with pride as, sitting next to Jassey, I watched her in her gown and mortar board, collecting her degree. The odds were against her, and look what she has achieved. After a spell living with her father, Maria has come home and at the weekends she, Joshua and I can escape into the country for a walk or a bike ride. I am giving them the childhood full of unconditional love that I wanted for myself. I've built us a safe little world, a sanctuary where I can retreat to recharge my batteries, ready for the work ahead.

34

Not long after I met Zainab I started doing shift work in the local refuges and what I saw there convinced me of the need for specialist provision. Women who end up in refuges have had their lives pulled up by the roots. If they are to survive, an anonymous hostel won't do; they need something familiar, something as close as possible to what they've known and lost. I'm thinking of women like Shazia, a young Muslim girl, brought up in Birmingham, who was taken to Pakistan 'for a holiday' aged fifteen and married to a cousin whom she didn't even meet until the ceremony. After the wedding her family flew home and although Shazia begged and pleaded to be allowed to return with them, they left her in Pakistan for several months. They wanted to be sure she 'formed a relationship' with her husband. She had no choice: he forced himself on her the day her family left. Shazia told him how unhappy she was but he didn't care; he made no bones about the fact that all he wanted was a passport into England. She was allowed home only when she had promised to go through the procedures necessary to bring him over here.

Back in Birmingham Shazia wrote to the British Embassy explaining her plight and begging for their help. She explained that she'd been forced to marry her husband and forced to fill in the forms sponsoring him to come to England. She sent the letter via a friend so her parents wouldn't know about it, but she never got a reply. In desperation, three weeks after the man she had grown to hate arrived in this country, Shazia rang the police and asked to be given safe escort from her parents' house. She packed some bags and hid them in readiness but when the police arrived, when her mother started screaming and wailing and begging her to stay, she didn't have the strength to go and get them. She left empty-handed.

When I first saw her – a couple of weeks after that happened – she was sitting on her bed with that blank, shocked look you see in newspaper photographs of refugees. She had turned her back on everything she had ever known or loved. She was many miles from home with nothing at all familiar in her surroundings. The first thing she said to me was, 'Do you know where I could pray?' She was trying to cling to the shreds of her identity and there was nothing in that refuge to give her any help.

Shazia reminded me of my sixteen-year-old self. She'd had that same traditional upbringing that leaves you so vulnerable and unprepared for real life; if you can't conform you can't cope. She had to feed herself in the refuge, but she wasn't sure how to do it. 'How many loaves of bread will I need, Jas?' she said. Like me before I ran away, she'd never gone to the shops without having been told what to get. Her uncertainty ran much deeper than what she should eat. 'I don't know who I am any more, Jas,' she said as we sat talking. She was looking straight at me and the fear and confusion I could see in her eyes took me right back down the years. 'I ran away because I couldn't be the person Mum wanted, but I don't know how to be anybody else.'

To my mind you didn't have to look further than Shazia to see the need for specialist Asian women's refuges. She was going to need so much support before she could rebuild her life. And I wanted her to be able to rebuild it as an Asian woman. Running away mustn't mean you have to shrug off your whole identity. Pull-back to the culture you grew up with is very strong. I'd learnt by then that turning your back on bits of it doesn't mean that you reject it altogether. I'm proud to be an Asian woman and I wanted Shazia to be able to come through her trauma and feel the same.

When my shift was over I went back to the Karma Nirvana offices and started making a list of people to talk to, people from the police, health and social services. I knew they wouldn't all be sympathetic, I knew the people already running refuges might see it as muscling in on their patch; after all, there's only so much funding to be had. But the thought of Shazia kept me going. Do you know what she said to me just before I left? I was walking out the door when she caught my arm.

'I ran away to be free, but now I feel I've swapped one prison for another.'

I approached the national charity Refuge and asked if they would be prepared to form a partnership with Karma Nirvana to set up an Asian women's refuge and they agreed. I envisaged one house large enough for eight women, but by early 2001 – when we were racing to submit a funding application before the April deadline – I resigned myself to the fact that I wouldn't find that in Derby. I re-worked the plans for our pilot project using four two-bedroom properties instead.

We had the support of the local housing association but some of the properties they offered us defied belief. More than once I walked through the front door and gagged because of the smell. I got used to walking round them with a scarf or a handkerchief pressed over my nose and mouth. I saw kitchens thick with grease, carpets infested with fleas, houses in which the window frames had rotted and fallen out, or the ceilings had collapsed because of damp. We saw houses where I couldn't imagine keeping a dead dog, let alone a woman in need of solace. But the deadline meant we had to decide and eventually I took a leap of faith and picked four.

The funding application was successful and as soon as the money came through the renovations started. It was all done properly; the houses were stripped out and made good top to toe and within sixteen months all four of them were looking fantastic. I know many of the women who contact Karma Nirvana fear that running away will mean living in a hovel – just like Jassey and I did – but these houses prove them so wrong. They've got gardens, blinds at every window, washing machines, furniture – all of it brand new. We even managed to scrounge some prints to brighten them up a bit and a few books and toys for the kids.

But to my mind the important things in those houses are the big cooking pots, the *chapatti* pans, the racks of Indian spices and, in the living-room, the area set aside for prayer mats. When I go into the kitchen of one of those refuges nowadays I'm enveloped by the smell of Asian cooking; it's a warm familiar smell that wraps itself around me like a quilt. That's what I envisaged when I began my fight for specialist provision.

We opened those four refuges in 2002. Each one was designed to house two women and their children and in that first year

Karma Nirvana provided emergency accommodation for fifty-two women and their children and had to turn more than one hundred and twenty-five others away. To me that was more than proof of need and I immediately started advocating specialist provision as a national project. It has been a slow process, but there is now an Asian women's refuge in Stoke-on-Trent and talk of one in Burton.

That was the start of moving my work beyond Derby and now, increasingly, I am campaigning across the country, talking to police officers, social workers and teachers about the issues facing Asian women in Britain. Almost everywhere I go I find such thirst for knowledge, and such need. Often I talk in schools and when I do, among the kids who approach me to ask questions at the end, there are invariably one or two hollow-eyed Asian girls who murmur, 'What you talked about . . . it's happening to me.'

The stories I've heard from the women who seek help from Karma Nirvana are echoed wherever I go. So many Asian women suffer at the hands of their families who hurt them in ways that a stranger never would. Their torment is invisible because honour-based violence happens behind closed doors, but it is there, creeping like a cancer through our society.

Not everyone is willing to accept this. Not long ago, in Derby, I was addressing an annual meeting of magistrates on the subject of murder in the name of honour. When I'd finished talking three men stood up, wanting to speak. Two were supportive but the third, a Muslim Pakistani, a respected leader within his community, said: 'I've lived in Derby all my life and I have never heard of anything like the issues you discuss. Who are you anyway? I've never seen you before. I think you are an impostor.'

He denied any knowledge of honour-based violence despite the much-publicized case of Rukhsana Naz who – just like him – lived in Derby all her life. She went to my old school, Littleover. Rukhsana was nineteen years old and six months pregnant when her mother sat on her legs while her brother strangled her to death. They did it because she refused to abort the baby she was carrying, and they suspected it was not fathered by the man she had been forced to marry when she was just fifteen.

Hers was just one of the 5,000 honour killings that take place, worldwide, each year.

Luckily the British authorities, who in the past have been caught up in a fog of ignorance and misplaced cultural and religious sensitivity, have started to acknowledge the problems that Asian women face here. Honour killings are now recognized as such. Two terrible cases were reported while I was writing this book. The brother and cousin of twenty-five-year-old Samaira Nazir stabbed her eighteen times before cutting her throat, because she wanted to marry for love. They made her little sisters watch them do it, and the two girls ended up spattered with Samaira's blood. Nineteen-year-old Arash Ghorbani-Zarin was stabbed forty-six times by the brothers of the girl who was carrying his baby, the girl with whom he planned to spend his life.

Of the four men directly involved with these murders three were under twenty. Older men often use young relatives to do their dirty work, but what frightens me is that the younger generation seem to feel even more strongly than their elders do about the subjugation of women. I heard that despite our dreadful legacy, one member of our family has often said, 'If I had a daughter who went out with a Muslim I'd chop him into little pieces and gladly do time for it.'

As director of Karma Nirvana I am pleased and proud to be able to play my part in addressing these threats to Asian women. I have been asked on several occasions to advise on issues facing the Metropolitan Police body currently reviewing 120 murder cases to see if they should be reinvestigated as honour killings. So far it has been deemed that at least twelve of them should. I have developed close links with the Forced Marriage Unit which was set up by the Home Office and the Foreign and Commonwealth Office and now deals with more than 250 cases each year, some of them involving girls as young as ten years old. I am also asked with increasing frequency to offer advice on cases of honour-based violence that are brought to court. On a continuing basis, I feel privileged that so many women trust me with their stories of pain, and the fact that I can be a tool in their healing process is something I never take for granted.

Although many British Asians condemn honour-based violence and are delighted at the way its prevalence is now being exposed, not all of them share this view. The work I do makes me an object of hatred to some people. Last year, on a Saturday night, I was curled up on the sofa watching television with Maria and Joshua when my mobile phone rang. 'Where's Nadia? We know she's with you; we found your number in her bedroom.'

I knew exactly who the woman was, and her icy rage turned my stomach cold. About ten hours previously her daughter Nadia had called me from their home in a prosperous town just south of London, her voice shaking with fear.

She had been kept prisoner in the house for the previous two years while her family arranged her marriage to one of her first cousins. She didn't go to school, she didn't see friends; she was sixteen and she never went anywhere alone. Her step-father had stuck nails and barbed wire along the top of the fence surrounding their property just in case she tried to run away.

She told me most of that later. At the time all she said was that she'd found my number in a magazine article, and she needed my help. With hundreds of miles between us all I could do was outline her options, but it must have given her some courage because two hours later she rang again.

'I've done it. I got out of the house. I've escaped and I'm in the high street, please help me.'

I did what I could. I persuaded her to ring the local police and I rang a friend of mine in the Metropolitan Police. He dropped what he was doing and drove out to find her. By the time he got there she was in the local police station, getting more and more hysterical as an officer tried to persuade her that the best thing would be to let him take her home. I thought, once again, how lucky I was with the police officer who first found me and Jassey. Once Nadia had convinced my friend of the danger she would now be in at home, he took her back to London and arranged refuge accommodation.

When Nadia's mother rang that night I denied all knowledge of her daughter and hung up, but I knew I wouldn't be able to deflect her that easily. An hour or so later my mobile rang again. It was a male voice, ugly and menacing. 'We know you live in Derby, we know people who could find your house quite easily. Tell us where Nadia is or you might find yourself chopped into little pieces.'

I was scared, and impressed as ever by the efficiency of the Asian network. Two calls later – in which my children and their schools were mentioned – I rang the police. By the end of that weekend a panic button had been installed in my house and an officer had left me with a list of precautions to try and ensure my safety, things like varying my route home and never getting out of the car without checking first.

Taking those precautions made me stop and think, but only briefly. There is so much to do that I know I will continue this work until my dying day. I am currently researching a Ph.D on honour-based violence and I am also working to establish a National Friendship Network.

The women brave enough to stand up for themselves and escape from families who bully, abuse and imprison them face disownment, immense sadness and loss. In fleeing their families, they are forced to leave behind the communities they grew up in, the faces and places they have known all their lives. These women need friends who will understand them and support them, who will be the background to their lives as they struggle to rebuild their identities. A pilot project for the National Friendship Network is now under way, shaped by the views of people who have contacted Karma Nirvana in the past. I persuaded the Forced Marriage Unit to fund the training in skills such as listening and confidence-building of nineteen people who will be the first friends/mentors in this network, and I am now back on familiar territory: chasing further funds to make my vision real.

Last week a woman called Usha came to Karma Nirvana. She was seventeen. Having been tricked into a marriage abroad when she was just fifteen she was then kept prisoner in her home in Stoke for more than a year while she saved to 'bring her husband over'. When the school's welfare officer came looking for her, Usha's mum would push her into the cellar and lock the door. She was always very polite to the welfare officer, offering her a cup of tea, grateful for her concern; inviting her to call again if she wanted to. 'It's just that Usha is not well today, she's sleeping,' she'd say. Or, 'Usha has had to go round to her auntie's to look after the children while Auntie takes Uncle to hospital.'

She was charming enough to convince the welfare officer that all was well and after a while she stopped calling. At first Usha tried to get help. She dialled 999 a couple of times, but when the police arrived at the door her mum would just say, polite as ever, 'Sorry, you must have got the wrong address. There's no one of that name here.' Then she'd beat Usha for making the call.

Eventually, like so many of us, Usha seized her chance and ran away. For the previous year she had been moving between bed and breakfasts, always on the run. By the time I met her she was in turmoil. She wanted to go home, but she was afraid of what would happen if she did. She had started self-harming, cutting herself. She showed me her thin forearm, criss-crossed with scars, some of them faded to faint silver lines but others still a vivid red. 'I don't want to do it; I feel really bad about it . . .' she said, struggling to look me in the eye. 'But it's the only way I can cope . . .'

In the months since she'd fled, wherever she sought refuge, her family had bombarded her with mobile phone calls. They used every trick they could think of to get her to come back.

'Your mum's got cancer . . .'

'Your uncle's died . . .'

'Your grandma's dying and she's asking for you . . .'

Every last iota of emotional blackmail was brought to bear and I knew that, despite all she'd been through, Usha longed to give in to it.

'I can't help it,' she whispered. 'I really miss my mum.' It's for women like Usha that I am determined to make this network happen. Friendship can never truly replace family but it helps, I know that. I was once where Usha is.

35

One cold grey morning towards the end of 2005 I found myself on a train trundling north towards Dundee University. I was going to address the law faculty on the subject of forced marriage and honour-based violence. I'd been invited to do so by Jim Haslam, professor in the university's school of accountancy, business and finance. He had read about Karma Nirvana in one of the papers and it touched a chord. He wanted to help me spread the word.

The lecture theatre was packed that morning. There was the expected crop of fresh-faced students, eager with their A4 note-pads. But Jim had opened the invitation out beyond the university and there were a score or more of adults; social workers and health professionals, a couple of men from the police.

I could give this talk in my sleep if I wanted to, the material is so much part of me. But it never fails to move me because the facts are so appalling. Did you know that the suicide rate among young Asian women in Britain is three times the national average? I believe that many of them, like Robina, are driven to kill themselves; it's just a cleaner, more convenient form of murder. I will never take for granted the suffering that so many of them have to bear.

I fill my talks with stories of women like Shazia. She has moved on from refuge provision now; she's got a boyfriend and a job. Hers is a success story, although she still grieves for her family with whom she's had no contact since the day she left home. I often talk about Chandi, an eighteen-year-old girl I met when the Forced Marriage Unit brought her back to Britain. When Chandi's family said she and her sixteen-year-old sister were going on holiday to Pakistan, Chandi took the precaution of telling a friend. 'Here's where I'm going. If I'm not back in a month tell the police,' is what she said.

With that quick conversation, Chandi saved herself. She had been in Pakistan ten weeks when representatives of the British Embassy in Islamabad arrived in the village to which Chandi had been taken and – amidst scenes of hysterical anger – removed her from her new in-laws' house. In all the chaos, her younger sister, already traumatized by her sudden move from a north London suburb to a remote rural village and the unwanted attentions of the man she had been forced to marry, panicked and refused to leave, much to Chandi's distress. 'Mira got seven As in her GCSEs, Jas, but she doesn't know that,' Chandi told me. 'She's stuck there sweeping the cement floor of her mother-in-law's house.'

When I finished talking that morning at Dundee University you could have heard a pin drop. Looking up and down the rows of faces they looked genuinely shocked. Then hands started going up and the questions started. 'Why isn't forced marriage a criminal offence?' 'What happens to the women when they get brought back?' 'What can we do to help?' I got the impression that a lot of them, particularly the adults who'd come in from outside, were appalled by the fact they'd been in ignorance about these things happening in Britain. Jim had set aside half an hour for questions but it wasn't nearly enough; they were so thirsty for information that I could have talked all afternoon.

Eventually, when I stepped onto the train that was going to take me back to Derby, it was packed, standing room only. Wedged up against one another in the aisle, it was easier to talk than not, and I found myself telling the man I stood next to what I'd been doing in Dundee. He had never heard of forced marriage or honour killings and, as I was explaining, I watched the colour drain from the face of the elderly man standing next to him; he went deathly white.

I apologized. 'I'm sorry if I've upset or offended you. I know it sounds shocking but, believe me, it does happen.'

'I know,' he said. He was looking at me so intently I was almost scared. 'One of my chemistry students, a brilliant Asian girl . . . She came from Bradford but she was studying where I used to teach, at Glasgow University . . . It was years ago. She was doing a Ph.D. I did a lot of work with her and, as the months went by, she started to confide in me.'

He was craning towards me, oblivious to the press of people round us. 'She told me that her parents had arranged a marriage for her, but she didn't want to see it through. She told me they had a lot of arguments but I thought, "So what?" Most students argue with their parents. Even when she said her family was going to kill her because she wouldn't marry the man they'd chosen I didn't take it seriously. I couldn't believe that would happen. All I said was, "If you're really worried you should go to the police."'

Guilt stained his face, but he looked me straight in the eye as he said, 'I did nothing to help her and a week later she was dead.'

He read about it in the newspapers, a far-fetched story even by Asian standards. One night at 3 a.m. the girl went downstairs to the family garage to change the tyre on her car. Apparently she did not use the jack correctly and it collapsed, causing the car to fall and crush her head.

It was reported as a tragedy, an accidental death.

Karma Nirvana can be contacted for support, advice or to give a donation at:

Unit 6
Rosehill Business Centre
Normanton Road
Derby
DE23 6RH
Tel: 01332 604098